HOW TO
ARGUE

HOW TO
ARGUE
THIRD EDITION

ALASTAIR BONNETT

ALWAYS LEARNING

PEARSON

Harlow, England • London • New York • Boston • San Francisco • Toronto • Sydney
Auckland • Singapore • Hong Kong • Tokyo • Seoul • Taipei • New Delhi
Cape Town • Sao Paulo • Mexico City • Madrid • Amsterdam • Munich • Paris • Milan

Pearson Education Limited
Edinburgh Gate
Harlow
Essex CM20 2JE
England

and Associated Companies throughout the world

Visit us on the World Wide Web at:
www.pearsoned.co.uk

First published 2001
Second edition published 2008
Third edition published 2011

ISBN: 978-0-273-74385-9

British Library Cataloguing-in-Publication Data
A catalogue record for this book is available from the British Library

Library of Congress Cataloging-in-Publication Data
Bonnett, Alastair, 1964–
   How to argue : essential skills for writing and speaking convincingly / Alastair Bonnett. -- 3rd ed.
      p. cm.
   Includes bibliographical references and index.
   "Smarten study guides"--T.p. verso.
   Previous ed.: 2008.
   ISBN 978-0-273-74385-9 (pbk.)
  1. English language--Rhetoric. 2. Social sciences--Authorship. 3. Persuasion (Rhetoric) I. Title.
   PE1479.S62B66 2011
   808'.042--dc22
                                                         2010052031

10 9 8 7 6 5 4 3 2 1
15 14 13 12 11

Typeset in 10/13pt Din Regular by 3
Printed in Great Britain by Henry Ling Ltd, at the Dorset Press, Dorchester, Dorset

Smarter Study Skills

Instant answers to your most pressing university skills problems and queries

Are there any secrets to successful study?

The simple answer is 'yes' – there are some essential skills, tips and techniques that can help you to improve your performance and success in all areas of your university studies.

These handy, easy-to-use guides to the most common areas where most students need help, provide accessible, straightforward practical tips and instant solutions that provide you with the tools and techniques that will enable you to improve your performance and get better results – and better grades!

Each book in the series allows you to assess and address a particular set of skills and strategies, in crucial areas of your studies. Each book then delivers practical, no-nonsense tips, techniques and strategies that will enable you to significantly improve your abilities and performance in time to make a difference.

The books in the series are:

- *How to Write Essays & Assignments*
- *How to Write Dissertations & Project Reports*
- *How to Argue*
- *How to Improve your Maths Skills*
- *How to Use Statistics*
- *How to Succeed in Exams & Assessments*

For a complete handbook covering all of these study skills and more:

- *The Smarter Study Skills Companion*

Get smart, get a head start!

Contents

Acknowledgements

I've had a lot of help with this book. The following have provided encouraging and constructive comments on earlier drafts: Will Allen, Andy Baker, Paul Bonnett, Raymond Bonnett, Shirley Bonnett, Rachel Holland, Nina Laurie, Anoop Nayak, Matthew Smith and Neil Ward. The responsibility for any errors in the final text rests, of course, with me.

Thanks also to Steve Temblett, Katy Robinson and Lauren Hayward at Pearson Education for their help and support with this revised edition.

How to use this book: Quick Route

How to Argue has been organised and designed to be as user-friendly as possible. Each chapter deals with a particular aspect of writing, presenting or assessment/exam technique. You can read the book through from end-to-end, or in sections, or dip into specific chapters as and when you think you need them.

At the start of each chapter you'll find a brief paragraph and a **Key topics** list, which lets you know what's included. There is also a list of **Key terms**.

Within each chapter, the text is laid out to help you absorb the key concepts easily, using headings and bulleted lists to help you find what you need as efficiently as possible. Relevant examples are contained in boxes, which can be consulted independently, if necessary. The inset boxes are of five types:

Smart tip boxes emphasise key advice to ensure you adopt a successful approach.

Information boxes provide additional information, such as useful definitions or examples.

Chapters One and Two are organised into Steps. The Step summaries sum up the main points of each Step in a clear and concise way.

At the end of each chapter, there's a **Practical tips** section with additional tips. You should regard this as a menu from which to select the ideas that appeal to you and your learning personality.

There are **Exercises** for you to do by yourself or in a group, which test whether you have understood the chapter, and give you an opportunity to put what you have learnt into practice.

Introduction

● How not to argue

Most of us have learnt how not to argue. We have learnt how to avoid getting involved, how to escape being drawn in. It seems the safe option, the easy path. For a while. Until the awful day when our escape route turns out to have led to the most controversial and outrageous position of all, of not caring. With horrible irony we find ourselves staunch supporters of the most stupid argument of them all. The lesson is clear: there is no such thing as not having an argument. The choice before us is not whether to argue but whether to do it well. This book shows you how to meet that inevitable challenge. It will explain how to build an argument and how to engage with the arguments of others.

The ability to engage in argument is what makes learning exciting. To feel comfortable with debate changes your relationship with education and just about everything else. It transforms you from a passive and bored receptacle of another's wisdom into a participant; into someone who is neither scared by, nor indifferent to, the society around them but actively involved in its interpretation and transformation.

Most students in higher education find the idea of having to argue daunting. This feeling isn't helped by the fact that professors and college lecturers often provide feedback on student essays that commences with a long silent stare at your script and concludes with the observation, 'There's lots here but there's no argument' or 'This is merely descriptive'. At this point new students often become baffled. What is an argument? What is 'mere' about description? These are good questions. Unfortunately they rarely get adequate answers. For although arguing is vital for success in most disciplines, the skills and culture of academic argument are rarely clearly introduced to students. This is particularly perverse, since it is the expectation that university students are being taught how to participate in debate which sets them apart from students in other forms of education. Indeed this expectation is commonly taken to represent the single most important indication of a student's progression from secondary to tertiary education. It's no wonder that lecturers and professors feel so strongly about the subject and that they identify good students as ones who demonstrate the ability to argue, and weak students as ones who don't. It's just a shame that more is not done to disabuse students of the notion that there is something terribly difficult or mysterious about getting into the former category.

An academic argument is a tool of learning and understanding. It is a form of intellectual **engagement**, a constructive intervention designed to contribute to a debate. As this implies, academic argument is a type of **exchange** based on a sharing of knowledge, a pooling of facts and opinions. It is – or at least it should be – restless, unsettled, always trying to move forward. Such ideals are diametrically opposed to the notion that the point of arguments is to win them, that argument is all about personal domination. Thus the book in your hands has very little in common with top lawyer Gerry Spence's *How to Argue and Win Every Time* (1995). If you want to 'become born-again gladiators' then Gerry is the man for you. Not that he battles alone. The conviction that arguments are and should be about merciless combat is widespread, being particularly prevalent within 'self-help' resources that claim to be able to make everyone a 'winner'. This kind of stuff conjures up an image of the successful arguer as a sharp-suited, square-jawed, horribly handsome person with a steely glint in their eye; the kind of clever and ruthless bully that frightens the life out of most of us. This terrifying figure appears to be an amalgam of lawyer, politician and business leader. Powerful people. But, as much as we may admire their verbal dexterity, offering such folk as model arguers is profoundly unconvincing. They may provide absorbing spectacles of debate but there is something self-serving and intellectually dead about their approach to argument; more specifically, in their desperation never to lose. Indeed, despite its apparent popularity, the dog-eat-dog approach to argument – in which the most vicious animal gets to sit on the stripped bones of its opponent – is a singularly bad way of taking part in a debate or learning anything.

Although academics usually don't live up to their own high ideals, there is something uniquely valuable about the way argument is understood in higher education. What I will be calling good argument in this book draws on skills of learning, listening and communication. It is a form of involvement; a willingness to participate actively in the pursuit of intellectual insight and knowledge. Let no one imagine that this model of argument is a soft option. It is true that it isn't gladiatorial. It is unlikely you will lose any limbs. Yet, in contrast to the mock heroics of more aggressive approaches, it is not simply a performance. Our modern gladiators – those bullish battlers who are forever locking horns in the law courts, boardroom, or on the television news – play their games, fight their pretend wars, then walk away with a wink. The path we shall be following in this book makes much greater and more serious claims on all parties involved. The most fundamental of all is that one argues because one believes something to be so and to be worth saying. This doesn't mean that you have to search the darkest reaches of your soul every time you want to make a point. What it does mean is that what you argue is what you stand for, what you care about. Thus it is necessary to ask oneself, not just once but many times, 'What, on balance, do I believe to be true?' and 'What really matters here?' These aren't questions that can be answered simply or glibly. They are infuriating questions. Sometimes the appropriate answer may seem like 'Nothing', and very often 'I'm not sure'. But the questions need to remain, as nags, as irritants that can never be scratched away.

Argument is not simply a 'transferable skill'. It isn't something to be ranked alongside computer literacy and time management. The ability to argue in an informed and constructive way is the core attribute of all forms of advanced level education. But it's more than that too. For argument goes to the heart of who we are and what we want to do with our lives.

The art of the plausible: argument in the real world

There are many professions in which the ability to construct a rational and informed argument comes in very handy. Whether you are proposing new policies or products, or defending existing ones, you need to be able to understand why some arguments are more plausible than others. There are lots of combative models of argument out there to tempt the bullish. But what would you find more convincing? A reasoned case that acknowledged and engaged with counter-argument and counter-evidence, or a polemic? I'm not pretending that the academic approach can or should be simply parachuted into more 'normal' situations. Much of the subtle toing and froing between numerous different perspectives, not to mention the nerdy glee at the sight of pendulous bibliographies, that characterises academic interventions can appear ponderous in the real world. However, stripped down to their essentials, the skills introduced in this book could be useful in many different contexts. Thinking about the form and quality of an argument, about its thoroughness and limitations, can help anyone both achieve their immediate goals and communicate with intellectual integrity and confidence.

Arguments are to be avoided; they are always vulgar and often convincing.

(Oscar Wilde)

Getting started

The first steps in developing your argument

This chapter takes you through the **three key steps** you need to take *before* you can deliver your argument. It explains why you must ask yourself a simple but tough question: 'Does it matter?' (Step 1). If your argument is a 'substantive' one then it is time to consider the form or type of argument you will deploy (Step 2). Six different types of argument are introduced to help you make this decision. Finally, you will need to write down a rough version of your argument (Step 3). You will then be in a position to begin structuring it into a written or oral form that is plausible and effective (Ch 2).

Key topics
- Does it matter?
- Choosing your argument

Key terms
substantive arguments   types of argument   summarising

It is an uncomfortable moment. You haven't written a word. The screen is blank. Your notebook is empty. And you have to develop an argument. You have to perform a feat of illuminating intellectual pyrotechnics when your brain feels like it couldn't sustain even the most spluttering of budget sparklers. This is how it always is. This is how it begins.

All you start with is one stark fact: that without a good argument all your skills of communication and presentation, the sophistication of your spellchecker and the neatness of your binding, will count for a mark too depressing to contemplate.

The first things to remind yourself are that it's like this for everyone and that developing an argument is not that hard. There is no mystery to it. Indeed it is something within everyone's grasp to do and do well. Almost invariably when students are instructed to develop an argument they are being asked to demonstrate their **familiarity**, their **capacity to engage,** with established ideas and existing debates. Producing a good argument has very little to do with staring off into some elusive, misty distance for inspiration or tapping into the emotions of your inner child. The truth is more prosaic. And a large part of that truth is that strong arguments need work. The brutal reality is that the sooner you start writing and shaping your argument the better it will be. This chapter will show you how to begin that process.

Don't forget, if you're in a terrible hurry you can speed your way through this and subsequent chapters by consulting the quick route through the book on p. ix.

> Make *lots* of notes. Good arguments emerge from a profusion of ideas, a clutter of thoughts. From the moment your brain slips out of neutral and is clunked into first gear you need to be making notes, scribbling stuff. The more you write, however feeble, obvious or plain silly it may seem at first, the more sophisticated and exciting the final product will be.

● Step 1: Does it matter?

This is where bad arguments begin. Not with faulty logic or inaccurate facts but with something much more basic. One of the most common comments markers make on exam and project scripts is the pithy and devastating 'So what?' **'So what?' spells doom**. It means that this essay isn't saying anything, that it is wasting the time of everyone involved. Comments in the margin that are equally concise and almost as lethal are 'obvious' and 'merely descriptive'. These death knells all derive from the same assumption: that students are expected to produce a **substantive engagement with substantive issues**. But what does this mean?

A substantive argument deals with either:

● A core concern within an ongoing debate in your area. Within the literature in your field you will find that certain authors, terms and ideas crop up repeatedly and form the axes of debate. Substantive arguments arise from an engagement with these established and recognised reference points.

Or:

● An issue that *should* be a core concern within your field. This is a bolder departure point. Rather than sticking to what is already established as important within your particular area of interest you can look outside and draw in topics, ideas and authors that have been overlooked, unappreciated and, more important, have a contribution to make to existing debates in your area.

A substantive argument is *always* focused and precise. The more clearly and exactly you can pinpoint the issue that your argument is going to tackle, the more useful and informed your argument will be. Substantive arguments cannot be vague arguments. Sometimes this means that good arguments appear highly confined, restricted and qualified. However, in academic debate this is not considered a bad thing. To have something precisely formulated means that it is likely to be clear and constructive.

A substantive argument is not:

● About a mere detail. Using a minor illustration to engage bigger themes can be a useful technique. However, if you don't make this step, if you stay dawdling with questions and topics that are best consigned to footnotes, then examiners will start wondering, 'Why does this matter?'

● About anything and everything. Pitching your argument at too great a level of abstraction renders it just as meaningless as if it was concerned with an inconsequential detail. If you're in doubt about whether your starting point is too general or too particular, it is wise to stick closely to the key terms and ideas that have been established within your particular area of debate. The latter is a safe port: you won't chart new lands but you are also unlikely to get lost or run aground.

● Just about you. How much personal material is considered appropriate varies widely between different courses and markers. If you are going to draw on such material you need to check that it is acceptable. However, even when it is allowed or encouraged you need be wary of **solipsism** (see Glossary) or of using personal testimony as a substitute for engaging with the literature.

- Merely descriptive. When markers are looking for argument, 'description' often gets the prefix 'mere'. This always seems outrageously harsh to those students who have collected huge lists of facts and expect their labours to be rewarded. However, without a framework with which to interpret them, facts do not constitute an argument. Facts do not 'speak for themselves'. They need to be analysed, explained and provided with a context. Otherwise they are, quite literally, meaningless.

- Plain obvious! Reaffirming uncontroversial basic propositions is the royal route to a low or middling mark. It may get you through an exam (although this is no certainty) but there are plenty of more interesting ways this can be done, ways that make life as a student much more rewarding.

Examples of substantive argument

To help us to think about the qualities of substantive argument I've invented some examples. The first set of arguments below would be regarded as substantive (if not necessarily accurate), the second set would elicit the remark 'So what?' You will note that the statements in the first list suggest an appreciation of complexity while those in the second list do not. This attribute is, in part, communicated by the fact that the first set of arguments do not propose a black and white view of the world: their claims are qualified and contextualised, not simplistic and mono-dimensional. There also exists a distinction between the type of argument presented in each list. The first set of arguments offer an analysis – they promise to provide an explanation of a phenomenon. The second set, by contrast, are descriptive – they promise little more than the itemisation of facts. The examples are also all illustrations of the use of the key sentence in any essay, the one that typically commences, 'In this essay I will argue that ...'

Substantive

In this essay I will argue that:

- neo-Malthusianism remains a viable and accurate model of world population growth;
- the most profound consequences of the French Revolution were felt in Haiti;

- the utility of the two principal techniques currently employed to ameliorate or prevent desertification can only be fully exploited when they are allied to a range of other, supplementary measures;
- the British economy in the nineteenth century was not a laissez-faire economy and that the idea that it was is a politically motivated myth;
- the state management of ethnic diversity in China evidences considerably more flexibility and sophistication than critics of the system have often allowed.

'So what?'

In this essay I will argue that:

- the population of the world is increasing rapidly;
- the French Revolution was highly significant;
- there are 16 ways to prevent desertification;
- the British economy became more industrialised in the nineteenth century;
- China is an ethnically diverse society and that there are 13 major ethnic groups.

 Step 1: Summary

Be bold!

Go for the big questions, the substantive issues.

● Step 2: Choosing your argument

In this section I introduce six types of argument. Having acquainted yourself with Step 1 you can look through the list and see which is suitable for your purpose. This list is designed to help you survey your options and make an initial choice. It does not provide comprehensive introductions to any of the arguments covered. Introductory reading on each of the types of argument sketched below is provided in the further reading section at the end of this chapter.

Before going any further it is worthwhile considering what arguments do, what function they perform in debate. The arguments presented here provide different structures of explanation, structures that can be used as frameworks in which to develop specific theories. They also provide ways of making the case that an idea is 'wrong' or 'biased'. However, it is important to understand that, on their own, such accusations are feeble substitutes for argument. Only when they are the culmination of clear and logical investigation do they serve any kind of scholarly purpose. In fact the forms of argument provided here are not designed to produce or encourage crude pejorative statements or, indeed, ringing endorsements. Rather, they provide ways of sustaining the assertion that one is **understanding** and **constructively engaging** with one's material.

Of course, you may not find what you are looking for here. After all, argument is as multifaceted as the human imagination. However, within academic debate certain patterns keep cropping up. Certain formulations have been found to work and have come to represent what we may call 'legitimate modes' of academic debate. My typology is designed to reflect the main, recognised forms of argument current within higher education. The arguments presented are not equivalent, in the sense of delivering the same level of logical robustness. However, all are capable of providing a convincing intellectual structure for most undergraduate assignments.

Students need arguments because students are asked to **analyse things**. The argument you adopt is going to depend on the nature, quality and, perhaps, quantity of those things. I have provided some guidance on what kind of data or material each of these six arguments is most suitable for. However, these are merely general tips designed to encourage you to think about the applicability of each argument. To offer a more rigid framework, one that attempts to map out precisely which types of argument 'go with' which types of data, would be to stymie the essentially creative process you are embarked upon.

You may use this section in one of two ways. I've mentioned one already: when confronted with an essay title you may simply go through the list and pick out an appropriate argument. A different way of using this section is to use its contents to identify the arguments found within the material that you are working on. In other words you can use the classifications provided to discuss the nature of somebody else's argument. Such an approach enables you to depict but also to criticise arguments (see Chapter 4 for more help with this).

As this implies, each of the six arguments outlined here has its limits. They each enable an argument to be made but they also impose boundaries and blinkers. Each argument is better at 'seeing' some things than others, is more sophisticated in one domain than another. What structures and enables also confines. Once we understand this, a fundamental lesson of rigorous academic argument comes into view: you can't do everything! Good arguments are not ones that claim to be all-seeing and all-knowing. Even the most ambitious of theories only works, only functions satisfactorily, when applied to 'appropriate' material.

When offering an argument it is important not to promise too much, not to pledge perfection and deliver disappointment. My advice when using any of the arguments discussed below is not merely to know their limits but to be prepared to spell them out for your readers. Let them know that your approach cannot engage or provide answers to certain questions. Let them know that you appreciate what your argument is capable of and what it is unable to do.

At the end of each section or subsection I've provided some illustrative sentences. These are designed to help you translate your ideas into the kind of succinct summary statements that will impress your markers. I've often made mention in these little sentences of the names of authors (the names and achievements of whom are pure invention). I've done this to remind readers that academic arguments represent engagements with existing scholarship.

Just because arguing well isn't beyond anybody doesn't mean that the examples below are all as easy as slipping off a wet barrel. Some of them take practice and patience to appreciate and apply. Those forms that seem, at first glance, to be more demanding are addressed **first**. This should not be taken to imply that these forms are better or will necessarily lead to more rewarding and sophisticated arguments. Often simpler forms are the most effective and plausible.

Argument 1: Identifying tensions

This is a classic. Ninety-nine markers out of a hundred are impressed by it (and the one who isn't probably wouldn't be impressed by anything). Academics are attracted to themes of contradiction, tension and conflict because their elucidation demands a certain level of intellectual confidence and subtlety. Students who develop an eye or ear for this type of argument can easily find themselves being regarded as promising scholars.

To identify a tension within a process or event is to identify a point of strain between its constituent parts. Thus, at a minimum, one needs to be able to pinpoint three things: the site of conflict, and two things that are in conflict. Although it is often necessary to discuss multiple and connected tensions it is important to have a central focus, a prioritised site of interest. It is therefore advisable to limit the number of substantive tensions you are claiming to analyse. Even within a lengthy project any attempt to deal with over four or five will probably end in confusion. Normally one or two is enough.

'Tension' is a broad and inclusive term. Under its umbrella may be found a variety of more specialised approaches. Two of the most important of these – contradiction and deconstruction – are addressed below. However, using the more general concept of tension (and overlapping ideas such as conflict, friction and disjunction) is often useful precisely because it is relatively non-specific. It enables students to discuss the existence of a state of strain between things without having to identify those things as inherently incompatible (i.e. contradictory) or claim to be applying the techniques of deconstruction.

Useful phrases

In this essay it will be argued that:

- the work of Saunders exhibits a tension between ... and ...;
- two principal tensions can be identified in the work of Wieviorka ...;
- the conflict between ... and ... within ... subverts its overall ambition to ...;
- the tension identified by Martin in the work of James is exaggerated;
- without the existence of a disjunction between ... and ... in the work of UNESCO they would not be able to ...;
- Brah manages the tension between ... and ... within her work by ...

Contradiction

Students need to be careful about being too free with the term contradiction. It is often used rather loosely, as if it simply meant the same thing as tension. However, the real value of the idea of contradiction only emerges when it is understood to refer to a *special type* of tension. When it can be shown that two statements, themes or processes **directly oppose one another** then we may speak of the existence of a contradiction. As this implies, when discussing contradictions it is important to do more than simply identify the point and sources of conflict. It is also necessary to explain why the forces under discussion are opposites.

To illustrate what is distinctive about contradictions, let's look at an (entirely fictional) example from international politics. When considering European Union foreign regional policy, imagine that you have noticed that, in Africa, it supports protectionism while, in Asia, it places emphasis on the development of the free market. You have identified two different approaches in two different parts of the world. There may exist a tension between these two policies, but they are not inherently incompatible. There is no necessary contradiction between them. However if one was able to show that the European Union had a global foreign policy that committed it, ethically and ideologically, to the worldwide dismantling of protectionism, then a contradiction could be identified between its global and regional claims and ambitions. Moreover if, at a more detailed level of analysis, one was able to reveal that the European Union was encouraging Asian economies to invest and intervene in African markets, then another contradiction would be exposed. Such a situation would suggest a failure of clarity and purpose within European Union foreign policy.

One can identify contradictions in all sorts of places. In economic policy, in novels, in cultures; wherever you look you will find them. Moreover, since contradiction implies an unsustainable and crisis-prone situation (and, therefore, one that is inherently difficult both to admit to and to resolve), its examination can often be usefully accompanied by the consideration of the ways its existence is concealed or made to seem unproblematic.

The identification of contradictions is sometimes associated with dialectical thinking. Dialectics is a word that often confuses people. This is hardly surprising since it has two meanings. It was, originally, another word for argument or logical dialogue. This sense of the term reflects its roots in ancient Greek philosophy. However, its other meaning is more specific and, hence, of more use to students. For dialectics also refers to the identification of a **contradictory process**. More precisely it refers to three things:

1. Something (a thesis).
2. Its opposite (an anti-thesis).
3. The synthesis of this contradiction. Thus to call something dialectical is to identify a movement from thesis and anti-thesis to synthesis.

The best-known example of dialectical thinking is the Marxist theory of dialectical materialism. Marx took the idea of dialectics and applied it to socio-economic change. Traditional Marxists claim that there exists a dialectical momentum between the economic relations between people (the relations of production) and the historical and technological context of production (the forces of production). The contradiction between these two things achieves its synthesis in social crisis and change. However, the concept of dialectics can be applied in many different contexts. In any situation where one can identify a contradiction between something and an opposing force, a contradiction that has led or is leading to a third position, a synthesis, then one can describe both this process and one's argument as dialectical.

Deconstruction

Although a relatively recent concept, deconstruction has become a familiar form of argument in the humanities and, to a lesser extent, the social sciences. Like contradiction, it is a term that is often used loosely. Yet to use deconstruction as a synonym for tension or conflict is to waste its potential. It is a specialised term with a specific function. While other ways of arguing about tensions look at the relations between things, but take the meaning of those things for granted, deconstruction is concerned with the inadequacy of one's categories of analysis. Thus it is especially good at 'opening up' ideas that other forms of argument pass by. More specifically, it provides students with the tools to develop an immanent criticism of established notions (for example, 'man', 'employment', 'race') and traditions.

The focus of deconstruction is upon:

● the internal conflicts within its object of enquiry;

● the inevitable failure of anything to have a fixed or final meaning.

In the view of the deconstructionist the notion that any idea or category is permanent or stable is a pretence. Thus, deconstruction seeks to expose the way ideas are constructed and defended in the context of a continual 'spilling away' of meaning, its continual 'failure' to be self-reliant. Deconstruction arose from philosophy and, as the last sentence perhaps exemplifies, is often discussed in dense and highly abstract language. However, the power of deconstruction to 'break open' established categories and subject them to an internal critique makes it a useful intellectual device and one that it is often worth persevering with.

Useful phrases

In this essay it will be argued that:

● there exists a contradiction between ... and ...;

● the contradiction between ... and ... remains unresolved;

● the contradiction between ... and ... cannot be resolved by ...;

● there exists a dialectical momentum in the work of Miller;

● the idea of 'Europe' needs to be deconstructed;

● the repressed and marginal category in ... structures the narrative.

When building an argument that is based on the identification of tensions the key to success is not the number of tensions you can spot but their precise definition. Keep the number of factors in play to a minimum and make sure they are clearly defined early on.

Argument 2: Cause and effect

To say that one thing causes another can be a statement of fact. But it is always also a claim, an assertion that we can take issue with or revise. Indeed, as a general rule, it is better to think of claims of causation as something to be considered in the light of supporting evidence rather than as 'obvious' or 'common sense'.

There are three main ways arguments can engage issues of causality:

1. One may locate a causal relationship within one's subject matter.
2. One may attempt to locate an issue (for example, a mistake) within a causal relationship claimed by somebody else.
3. One may apply either inductive or deductive logic to one's evidence.

This last topic is a complex one and has been given its own section in this list (Argument 3). For now we will focus our attention on the first two uses. Each can supply extraordinarily powerful and creative arguments. However, there exist a variety of ways that each is interpreted. A common distinction is between qualitative and quantitative approaches. These are not incompatible, indeed most work in the social sciences combines them. However, they do represent different methodologies, a dissimilarity that is, in large part, a reflection of differences between both the kinds of material they are applied to and the claims made on its behalf. We may summarise this distinction as follows:

- **Qualitative explanations of causality** address non-numerical data (policies, discourses, events) and seek to arrive at a rational explanation of the relationship between them.
- **Quantitative explanations of causality** address sets of numerical data and seek to arrive at a statistical indicator of the nature of the relationship between them.

Your choice of approach (qualitative, quantitative or both) will be heavily influenced by your discipline. English literature doesn't have a strong tradition of statistical analysis; economic geography, by contrast, has traditionally made little use of qualitative procedures. However, whichever subject you are studying, it is useful to keep an open mind to the advantages of either approach. Let us not forget that statistics are not dropped from heaven; they come from people, and from the categories and processes of collection that people have developed. For example, in social surveys I am often classified as 'white', a category that is then transformed into a statistic and fed into various mathematical models. Yet the way racial classification is conducted, the categories used, and the fact that it is conducted at all, are not uncontroversial or natural facts. They reflect a particular history and way of viewing the world; matters of considerable importance that disappear from view in purely statistical approaches. On the other hand, it is reasonable to ask how a purely qualitative approach could ever make sense of its material. After all, the idea of number is present every time we say something has a frequency, that it is being repeated, that it occurs often, or never, or always. Quantification cannot be shoved off to the sidelines, as if it represented some remote scientific paradigm, any more than qualitative judgements can be removed from the process of classification.

Arguments about causes that use qualitative evidence

When you wish to argue that something has caused something else you need to explain how and why. Moreover, if your source material is qualitative in form then you will need to provide sufficient evidence for your claim to appear plausible. The question thus arises: 'What is "sufficient evidence"?' A distinction can be drawn between a claim for a causal relationship that supports or reiterates the work of an authority in your field and one that is original. In the former case the burden of explanation is far less. If the reliability and status of your authority is widely accepted then any further evidence that you provide is supplementary and, hence, can be sketched quite lightly. By contrast, if you wish to strike out on your own, and reap the benefits of being regarded as original, then you will have to work much harder.

To establish a plausible and convincing relationship between things you need to:

- look for any counter-evidence and engage with this in your argument;
- support the claimed relationship with a broad range of evidence;
- indicate clearly what kind and strength of relationship you are claiming.

The last point requires some explanation. The more complex one's material, and the less amenable it is to quantification, the more wary one should be of claiming to have discovered unproblematic and objective processes of causality. To put it another way, qualitative approaches use a lot of qualifying words and phrases, such as 'tend', 'in part' and 'to some extent'. Thus the claims of causality that are made are explicitly limited.

Let's take an example from anthropology. Say a study of emigration among Algerian peasant families has collected in-depth interview data from 30 families, data indicating that the inflexible and conservative nature of the tenant farming system has played a role in encouraging people to leave the country. There is no 'scientific' proof provided here. However, what one can say is that, having taken into account a range of evidence, farming tenancy and emigration can and may be linked. In such a study one would probably want to consider the explanations the interviewees provided of this phenomenon. However, one would also want to be hesitant about distinguishing too clearly and simply between cause and effect: all the factors involved may be mutually enforcing. Qualitative approaches are especially good at opening up the interconnected nature of causes and effects. A related characteristic is that they often shy away from claiming to have identified a single cause for things: life is usually more complex than that.

Locating a mistake within a causal relationship claimed by someone else means you are asserting either:

(a) that the claim that x leads to y is wrong because it is impossible (and, perhaps, illogical);

(b) that the claim that x leads to y is wrong because it does not (the link may be possible under certain circumstances but they do not prevail); and/or

(c) that the claim that x leads to y is not wrong but the relationship is described inaccurately.

The first of these charges is the more damning of the three and the rarest. Its most useful application occurs when you are able to show that data have been misunderstood (for example, x cannot lead to y because there is no such thing as y).

For a simple illustration consider the following sentence: 'Because Stephen's work is suffused with the romanticism of his times he often fell prey to a conservative apoliticism'. If you can show that Stephen's work is not 'suffused with romanticism' then the causal relationship claimed in this sentence falls apart. At this point it would be appropriate to find other explanations of the 'conservative apoliticism' alluded to. Alternatively, if you agree that Stephen's work was 'suffused' in the way described but wish to argue that it did not lead to 'conservative apoliticism' (i.e. employ argument b) then you would need to evidence the absence of 'conservative apoliticism' within his work and provide explanations of why it does not necessarily arise from romanticism. A third approach would be to take issue, not with the fact of the relationship described, but with the way the relationship is portrayed (i.e. to employ form c). A good place to start is with the inferences carried by particular words. For example, the phrase 'fell prey' suggests that Stephen was a passive victim of apolitical conservatism rather than an active agent, thus absolving him of any responsibility for the ideology.

Useful phrases

In this essay it will be argued that:

- ... was a key factor in the development of ...;

- ... is unlikely to have led to ...;

- the evidence that ... resulted in ... is equivocal and open to other interpretations;

- Home's analysis of the causes of ... fails to appreciate ...;

- Tompsett's analysis of the development of ... relies on a misconception of ....

Arguments about causes that use quantitative evidence

The first issue to consider in quantitative analysis is one of quality, namely 'What is the quality of one's data?' Are they reliable, up to date, expressed in the appropriate form, continuous? Where doubts concerning any of these issues occur they need to be acknowledged and accounted for. This will usually involve you in describing the process by which the data were collected and summarising its reliability. Depending on your discipline, such issues are then either bracketed off and treated as marginalia or integrated into your analysis as a core component of the whole.

Simple calculations, such as working out a mean, a weighted mean, a median or standard deviation, may give clues as to the existence of causal relationships. However, the three ways in which numerical data are most commonly employed to provide answers to questions of cause and effect are probability analysis, correlations and regression trends. Although the details of how to calculate these tests lies beyond the scope of this book (see the further reading section at the end of this chapter) they are presented here as potential resources, tools of analysis that can play a supporting or key role within arguments claiming to explain causal relationships.

Statistical indicators do not provide explanations. They are essentially descriptive. However, they can be very useful at suggesting explanations and indicating the strength of relationships. They show the relative strength of association between things and do so in a way that is clear, succinct and comparable with similar calculations. As always with issues of causality, whether qualitative or quantitative, you have to interpret your data carefully and admit to its limitations. When used in this way probability, correlations and regression analysis can be highly effective. Although you cannot prove a causal relationship with any of these techniques you can produce valuable evidence that will shed light on, or suggest the existence of, such a connection.

When arguing with numbers it is important to appreciate that something may be a statistical fact without it being either an accurate or useful reflection of reality. A critical sensibility to the valid use and potential abuse of statistics is always desirable. One of the best-known logical errors you can make in argument is to imagine that statistical relationships evidence causation. Just because you have produced a coefficient of 1.00 for the relationship between unemployment in Iceland and tomato production in the Philippines does not mean that one caused the other. Another potential problem to watch out for is the distortion that very high or very low numbers within one's range can create on the calculation of the whole set. It is often appropriate to ignore such 'outliers'. Such a decision, even if it involves discounting just a couple of figures, can radically change your final result. Distortion can also occur if one tries to derive a mean from an uneven data set. For example, if one's data have two peaks, one towards the bottom and one towards the top of their overall range, then any calculation based on their mean average is going to efface this 'bi-modal' pattern and, hence, introduce a possibly spurious element into your calculations. Yet another set of problems can occur from the practice of extrapolation (inferring the existence of points beyond one's data) or interpolation (inferring the existence of points between points within one's data). Predictions are not proofs. In order to be reliable they require the precise identification of the number and nature of relevant variables, something that is difficult, if not impossible, to achieve outside the natural sciences.

Probability analysis and significance testing

Probability analysis provides answers to the question: 'What is the likelihood of something happening by chance alone?' In order to answer this question statisticians employ a variety of models, each of which represents an ideal type considered appropriate for a certain type of data. The probability of an event is then calculated by considering how far it deviates from its expected position on the model. The three simplest models are:

1. **The uniform distribution model:** This is appropriate for considering situations where the likelihood of outcomes is the same; for example, throwing a die.

2. **The normal distribution model:** In graphic terms this model is bell shaped; it is considered to be appropriate for modelling probabilities for continuous data, for example the weight of British dogs.

3. **The binomial distribution model:** This is used when considering 'unpredictable' events with two possible outcomes, for example the probability that a baby at birth will be alive or stillborn.

Another area of statistics based on working out the likelihood of something happening by chance alone is significance tests. These are useful where you wish to argue that something has or has not had a significant impact on something else. More precisely, they allow you to assert that the existence of a causal relationship between them is likely or unlikely. There are a variety of such tests (for example, the z test and the binomial test) but they all require an initial hypothesis (a statistical claim that will be tested), a calculation of probability (known as the test statistic) and a decision to be taken on how rigorous the results need to be.

Correlations

Statistical correlations indicate the strength of the relationship between things. Correlation analysis produces correlation coefficients, a number between -1.00 and 1.00 (where -1.00 is a perfect negative correlation and 1.00 is a perfect positive correlation). There are various types of correlation calculation, different formulae being appropriate for different types of data, including linear and non-linear series and rank sets. For example, if a linear relationship is assumed then a calculation called the product–moment formula is appropriate. When only two variables are involved these calculations are called simple correlation. When more than two variables are being addressed then multiple correlation must be employed.

Regression analysis

This approach enables you to describe the nature of the relationship between sets of data and make predications based upon it. If you have two sets of data and you wish to describe and visually represent the relationship between them in numerical form then you can assign one set of data to the horizontal axis of a graph and the other to the vertical axis. You can then calculate a line of 'best fit' between your points. If your best-fit line is straight then this procedure is able to tell you whether a negative relationship (where one data set increases the other decreases) or a positive relationship (both increase or decrease together) exists between your sets of data and indicates the strength of this positive or negative association. If you have more than two sets of data then a more complicated, multivariate regression model is required. Regression analysis produces a description of a relationship. These descriptions can be used to develop or refute an analysis. They can also be employed to make predictions, either within the range of data you have (i.e. between the points or interpolations) or outside them (i.e. outside the points or extrapolations).

Useful phrases

In this essay it will be argued that:

- the relationship between ... and ... is not due to chance;
- Spivak's claim that ... caused ... is unconvincing;
- there is no significant relationship between ... and ...;
- Tey's notion that ... have increased as and because ... have decreased is unfounded;
- Champley confuses a correlation with causation;
- ... is likely in the near future to lead to ....

Rather than offer your own cause and effect argument it is often easier to critique someone else's. See Chapter 4 for more on how to do this.

Argument 3: Starting with observation or starting with an hypothesis

The arguments introduced in this section are sometimes considered the province of the natural sciences. However, they are also essential for anyone wishing to develop a theory from empirical data or, alternatively, test a theory 'against the facts'. The former is called induction, the latter deduction. In summary, induction is the process of arriving at a generalised conclusion on the basis of observation. By contrast, deduction is the process of arriving at a generalised conclusion by formulating a **thesis** or **hypothesis** (see Glossary), then testing it against empirical data.

Although both approaches are applied in all sorts of fields, their association with the sciences means that their employment in the humanities and social sciences often reflects a science-based agenda (i.e. the contention that these areas of study should become more scientific and less subjective). For many scholars scientific methodologies are seen as essential because they appear to be able to produce universal and objectively valid laws, based on universal and objectively verifiable facts. However, a sizeable group in the non-science disciplines (and an increasing faction within the sciences) have a very different understanding of the possibilities of induction and deduction. This group rejects the idea that objective facts are accessible and also tends to dispense with the aim of producing universal laws. Where induction and deduction are employed by such scholars they are used not to produce objective truths but better explanations; in other words to produce more sophisticated, more penetrating, more socially useful and, sometimes, more critical forms of understanding. Thus, although both positions are concerned with honesty and accuracy, the former group conceives of a good argument as, or as akin to, the discovery of a law of nature, while the latter sees good argument as a useful, workable and 'insightful' intervention.

From observation to theory

Trying to extrapolate theories from 'the facts' has a bad reputation. This is certainly the impression one gets from the most venerable illustration of inductive reason, the story of the white swans – a short but memorable tale. A study was once undertaken on the colour of swans. One thousand swans were counted. All those counted were white. The study concluded with a statement of law:

all swans are white. To well-travelled people such as ourselves, who have seen many a black swan, the logic here sounds obviously faulty. However, hasn't the very same logic convinced us of many things? That long plane journeys give you backache; that the sun is yellow; that winters are cold?

Clearly there is much room for error in induction. It is certainly not a recommended argument for those who wish to arrive at universal laws or objective theories. It cannot deliver these things. However, if we lower the level of our expectations, then induction does have its uses. Rather than extrapolating a universal law from the swan study, it would have been much more sensible to make a qualified, limited claim. If set within the context of the times, places and methods of the study, observing a thousand swans could legitimately form the foundation of an argument. The message is a simple one: inductive study is no good at producing universal laws but, once its limitations are known and communicated, it can be used to build other types of argument.

 Useful phrases

In this essay it will be argued that:

- the series of ... events at ... show that ...;

- ... incidents of ... in ... indicate that ...;

- the data we have on ... are erratic but support the contention that ...;

- new evidence of ... supports the claim that ...;

- ... lends weight to John's arguments that ...

From hypothesis to observation (and back to hypothesis): deduction

Science usually proceeds by way of experiment. It is an organic, hands-on process of trial and error; a way of investigating the world that can appear to have little need for methodological introspection. Despite this, the natural sciences are widely associated with a particular model of argument, a model that is respected and frequently employed in other fields. I am referring to argument by hypothesis. An hypothesis is a speculative proposition. It is not a truth claim but a testable starting point for an investigation or debate. Hypotheses can be sustained or disproved. This type of reasoning is known as deduction. It is usually preferable to induction because it is not reliant on a naive notion that 'facts speak for themselves'. Moreover, it allows for cumulative feedback between observation and theory. If you adopt this form of argument it is appropriate to include within your essay the following three elements:

- hypothesis
- evidence supporting and/or refuting your hypothesis
- revised hypothesis.

One of the strictest approaches to deduction follows the work of Karl Popper and is called falsificationism. As the term implies, falsificationism proposes that the only useful hypotheses are those that can be proved wrong. Popper thought that the theories of Marx and Freud failed this criterion, that they could never be verified or falsified; hence he regarded them as pseudo-science. In fact part of Popper's problem with Marx and Freud is that their theories are so complex that, while certain bits are amenable to falsification (for example the Marxist belief in the tendency for the rate of profit to fall within capitalism), taken as a whole they are incredibly adaptable, seeming to be able to explain away almost any eventuality. This may or may not be a problem with these two theories but it certainly reflects a flaw within falsificationism. After all, very few theories are so simple that one piece of counter-evidence warrants the destruction of the whole edifice. Indeed it is unlikely that either science or social science would have made any progress over the years if falsificationism had been adhered to. This becomes especially clear when we consider the fact that many of the established laws of natural science were developed in spite of the apparent existence of factual counter-evidence (for example, Newton's theory of gravity appeared to be falsified by the nature of the moon's orbit, while Copernicus's heliocentric model of the solar system was 'refuted' in his lifetime by observations on the movement of the stars).

The debate about testability and the role of theory in scientific argument is far from settled. However, one of the most important points that has emerged from this debate is relatively simple: deduction does not suit all types of evidence. It is particularly unsuitable for testing complex claims about social process and meaning. It is far better employed when dealing with simpler situations with a definite and limited number of variants. As this implies, the more precisely one can define the hypothesis to be tested the more convincing and logical one's choice of the deductive model of argument will be. It is also useful to recall the limits of falsificationism: the implications of inconsistent elements within your empirical data should not be exaggerated. One bit of counter-evidence does not necessarily mean that your hypothesis is wrong: there may be other explanations for this counter-evidence (indeed, it may itself be erroneous).

Useful phrases

The hypothesis that will be tested in this essay is that:

● wind power is not, at present, a commercially viable energy resource in western Europe;

● class consciousness is more pronounced among older male manual workers in Spain than among young male manual workers in Spain;

● acid rain is not the principal cause of the contraction of Scandinavian forests;

● despite the new evidence presented by Scutt, Banton's analysis of ... continues to be viable.

Stating your argument as a hypothesis can be useful whatever form of argument you end up using. Hypotheses are testable statements of fact and can provide a helpful component and a plausible starting point within many types of argument.

Argument 4: Arguing about words

This section looks at how one can develop an argument about words. More specifically, it addresses the way one may take issue with the way one or more of the key terms found within a debate are being used.

This form of argument requires that you identify an interesting, problematic or otherwise revealing key term or terms within your data. Sometimes this can be pretty easy. For example, if one was to analyse the policy and political documents produced by the post-1997 British Labour government one would encounter certain words standing out as catchphrases, words that are repeated and given a central place (for example 'modernise', 'joined-up thinking' and 'New Labour'). However, key terms often refuse to leap from the page quite so readily. Sometimes they are buried away, inconspicuously holding together a whole discourse. To return to the example of 'New Labour', we may note that the word 'socialist' looms large precisely because it is almost entirely absent. The key words that are not spoken can be as revealing as those that are.

Once you have identified the particular words or phrases that you consider revealing, the next step is to analyse them. This can be done in a variety of ways, but a useful initial distinction to make is between the definition and usage of a term.

Definition

A definition of the key term that you are considering may be provided within the material you are studying. In this case you may structure your argument around the analysis of the causes, context and adequacy of this definition. If more than one definition is provided this opens up further possibilities; more specifically one can compare their intent and identify tensions between them. When no definitions are provided it is often useful to concoct one or more of your own, noting that they are 'suggested', 'implied' or 'indicated' within your material.

Usage

How words are employed provides a huge variety of opportunities for interesting and original argument. Three approaches can be distinguished, each of which calls for a different level of engagement with the literature on language use. The first is the specialist approach, really only of concern to students within language studies and its cognate disciplines and need not detain us here. The second approach involves drawing on (as opposed to specialising in) a recognised tradition of language studies. The third may be summarised as an individualistic tack that makes no explicit claims to be following any particular tradition of language analysis. Students pursuing the second approach need to be aware of the resources and traditions at their disposal. More specifically, a basic grasp of the aim and utility of the following forms of language analysis is helpful:

● **Philology:** The study of the origins and changing use of words (also called etymology) and language.

- **Linguistics:** The study of language structure and use.
- **Sociolinguistics:** A branch of linguistics: the study of the relationship between language and society.
- **Discourse analysis:** This term has two principal meanings:
  - (a) a branch of linguistics that examines the way language is actually used in 'ordinary' contexts – a discourse is often considered to represent a stretch of language longer than a sentence;
  - (b) the study of the social and political development of different forms of categorisation and knowledge.
- **Semiotics:** The study of signs and signification systems (of any sort, including visual, cultural and so on).

Within the contemporary humanities and social sciences the most commonly employed approaches are sociolinguistics and discourse analysis (sense b). These broad and inclusive currents are particularly suited to social and political discussion and have the added advantage of being less technical than other forms of language study.

However, arguments concerning word usage do not have to invoke specialist literatures. It is worth noting that some of the most brilliant books in history and sociology concern themselves extensively with language use but make no mention of the manifold disciplines of language study. Indeed, if drawing on this literature is merely going to add confusing and tangential technical imports to your work it should be avoided. Within the humanities and much of the social sciences it is just as acceptable to make a clear statement explaining the particular way you are going to analyse a term or phrase and then get on with it. Four illustrative statements are provided below:

1. This essay will explore and explain the historical development of [the term or phrase].
2. This essay will explore and explain the existence of variations [either geographical or within a particular text] within the usage of [the term or phrase].
3. This essay will explore and explain the tensions [see Argument 1] exhibited within the use of [the term or phrase].
4. This essay will explore and explain the social and political function of [the term or phrase].

Writing or talking about words is one of the most productive and revealing ways of developing an argument. It does not require that you import masses of specialist linguistic terms into your field. What it does demand is some careful consideration of which terms are going to sustain a substantive argument and a clear statement of how you are going to analyse them.

Arguing about classifications

Classification is about label fixing. It is a necessary but also often a disputed process. What is a 'feminist'? Is Alberta 'rural'? Did Neanderthals have 'technology'? Was ancient Rome 'corrupt'? These are all questions which demand that a decision is taken about what is to be included within a classification.

Arguments about classification are common. Indeed in the humanities and social sciences new students often make the assignment of a classification to a particular individual, group or event their principal argument. There is nothing wrong with this. However, without a proper consideration of the classification that is going to be applied, it can lead to very banal conclusions. For instance, one student essay I remember marking offered the idea that Marx was a 'revolutionary' as its key argument. Needless to say, it didn't get many marks. After all, the author was merely stating the obvious. Being more particular, more focused, can sometimes rescue you from this kind of mistake. To argue that Marx was an 'Enlightenment revolutionary', a 'Eurocentric revolutionary' or even 'an armchair revolutionary', would be more specific and, therefore, potentially more insightful.

Two basic forms of classification arguments are introduced below.

They are/they aren't ...

When assigning a specific label to a person or thing, or refuting a classification applied to a person or thing, it is necessary to provide a definition of the label that you are employing. As I've noted above, this form of argument is particularly susceptible to truisms and dull formulations. If your classification appears to be in danger of being either then you probably need to make it more specific and/or draw in other authors to provide a variety of perspectives on the topic you are attempting to label. This approach also has the advantage of allowing you to evidence reading. Discussing someone else's classifications offers its own pitfall, however. Such an exercise can easily become merely descriptive. It is not sufficient to argue that 'Modood claims that Aziz is a functionalist'. You have to explain why she claims this and to assess the causes and appropriateness of this claim.

Changing and varying classifications

The historical, geographical and social diversity of classification provides plenty of opportunities for interesting argument. For example, what the label 'environment' meant 50 years ago, or what it means among different social groups today (nationalities, classes, ethnicities, etc.) may vary considerably from the standard definition employed within the contemporary natural or social sciences. Such variation can be highly complex and, where this is so, its 'mere description' may occasionally be legitimately offered as a substantive argument. However, it is always advisable to keep the 'Why?' question in mind and to apply it if there is any doubt as to the richness of the empirical data you are describing.

 Useful phrases

This essay will argue that:

- Ward's definition of ... leads her mistakenly to assume that ...;
- the ministry's statement is based on two, contradictory, definitions of ...;
- the history of the term ... provides a window on the changing economic fortunes of ...;
- the government's silence on ... evidences its unwillingness to develop an agenda on ...;
- Brandt may be classified as a ...;
- the categorisation of Amin as a ... is simplistic and misleading.

Words are important. But when using this type of argument we need to be particularly heedful of our initial question, 'Does it matter?' We need to make it clear why the particular terminological distinctions we are interested in are *significant*. Sometimes this can be done by showing there is a lively debate on the meaning of the words or classifications under review.

Argument 5: Contributions and impacts

Arguments 5 and 6, although strictly speaking subsets of our discussion on arguments about cause and effect, have, by their very ubiquity and popularity, a strong claim to be accorded their own discussion. In part, their widespread use may be explained by their alluring simplicity. To claim that x was a significant contribution to, or had a major impact on, y, is an apparently straightforward claim. The main dangers with this approach are oversimplification and a failure to identify adequately the precise nature of the 'contribution' or 'impact' under consideration. In the rest of this section I shall provide some pointers about the most effective way of employing this form of argument.

An argument is a form of analysis. When accounting for a contribution or impact it is not enough merely to state that it took place and that it was or was not important. You also have to provide an assessment of its particularity, its distinctiveness. Let's look at an example. Say you want to develop an argument concerning the contribution of an organisation called the Waterways Authority to the development of sustainable anti-pollution measures. Simply listing what the Authority did is not enough. Just claiming that its actions were important or significant doesn't help much either. Indeed, as a general rule, when you find yourself writing that a contribution or impact was 'big', 'small', 'significant', 'unimportant' and so on, pause and ask yourself, 'Have I explained why?' An analysis is more than a set of adjectives. On their own, adjectives merely pose more questions, such as 'Why was it important?' and 'What was significant about its contribution?' A more coherent argument about our hypothetical Waterways Authority and its impact on the development of sustainable anti-pollution measures could involve one or more of the following:

- A claim that the Authority's most widely recognised contribution is in a certain field but that you will argue that it has made a contribution (which is just as, or more, important) in another area.
- An assessment of the particularity of the Authority's contribution relative to other comparable authorities or bodies (see Argument 6).
- A detailed analysis of how the Authority's contribution was made; in other words, what mechanisms or processes need investigating before it can be fully explained.
- The application of Arguments 1 and/or 2.

In summary, arguments about contributions and impacts are enticingly straightforward and can be highly productive. However, they shouldn't be used as an excuse for mere description and oversimplification. Such arguments are not about listing facts but about explaining processes that change and challenge people, institutions and things.

Useful phrases

This essay will argue that:

- the EU's contribution to ... took the form of ...;

- the widely accepted assessment of the UN's contribution to ... is inadequate and misleading;

- the principal impact of ... lies in its ...;

- the impact of ... has been undermined by its own internal contradictions.

A good way to ensure that this type of argument does not end up looking descriptive is to combine it with a critique of somebody else's claims concerning contributions or impacts (see Chapter 4). Indeed, this is often an expected aspect of this type of argument. It is also the least demanding part: critiquing someone else's claims is usually easier than supporting your own.

Argument 6: Comparison and context

Comparison and contextualisation can illuminate all subjects. The two approaches have much in common. For example, both lend themselves to argument by counter-example, i.e. the strategy of refuting a particular position by reference to an instance that shows that it is wrong. Both can also suffer from the same problems, such as a lack of specificity about both the boundaries of the comparison or context and why they are being drawn. However, despite their similarities, these approaches have distinct aims.

Comparison

Comparative arguments analyse a phenomenon in the context of a separate but in some way similar phenomenon. One of the most popular forms of comparative argument is geographical, the comparison of one place with another. However, despite its ubiquity, the comparative method has some nasty pitfalls. The most important potential problems arise from a failure to answer adequately one simple question: 'Why are you comparing this with that?' Comparative arguments only work if they involve the examination of how things that are **held in common** vary in form within different contexts. They are concerned with *both* similarity and difference. Comparisons that assert that one thing is entirely different from another thing are pointless. The following points should assist in developing substantive and convincing comparative arguments:

- **Justify your choice of comparison.** This point may seem self-evident but it is shocking how little thought is often given to it. Within geographical comparisons arbitrariness can seem especially disconcerting – investigating a process in two or more regions or countries chosen at random from around the world is usually uninformative and often misleading.

- **Question your units of comparison.** Comparative approaches appear simplistic when they treat their units of analysis as natural and unproblematic. To take an example from communication studies, if you are comparing media institutions between different nations you need to attend to the fact that such institutions may not be nationally based (they may be local or transnational, for example). Moreover, even if we accept that it is useful, at some level, to write of the 'Indian media' or 'German media', this does not mean that these nations provide either an homogeneous or the most pertinent framework within which to understand the media activity within them. Treat your units as part of your analysis.

- **Focus down.** Always ask 'What is being compared?' The more specific and identifiable the thing or process that you are considering, the more useful your analysis will be. This point should also encourage you to keep the number of variables you are comparing to a minimum.

- **Identify relevant commonalities.** Comparative arguments only work when they show that something is shared, that something connects the units being contrasted. Again, the more specific your identification of this commonality, the better.

Context

All argument provides context. However, there exists a specific form of argument that offers contextualisation as its primary strategy.

Popular choices for contexts reflect the intellectual boundaries established by university disciplines (history, geography, politics, economics and so on). However, as with so many other forms of argument, the key to success with this approach is to be specific. The more precisely you can identify a revealing context, the more useful your argument will appear. It may be accurate to claim, for example, that 'This essay will argue that current anti-racist legislation in Malaysia can only be understood when placed within a historical context'. This statement might be useful as a general argument, but it needs to be swiftly supported by a more focused claim, such as: 'More specifically, it will be shown that it is rooted in the reaction of the government and commercial interests to the "race riots" of 1969'.

When discussing contexts it is tempting to keep widening one's parameters. As one learns more and realises that other material is relevant, the over-enthusiastic student will give in to the urge to just 'bung it all in'. The more astute might then make an *ex post facto* attempt to claim that their approach offers a 'large view' or 'wide sweep' of pertinent factors. However, sweeping up facts and vacuuming up details are random and unorganised methods and should be avoided in undergraduate assignments. Amassing contexts may suit the authors of foot-thick history books, but when you have fewer than 20,000 words at your disposal (and most student assignments are much shorter than this) trying not to 'leave anything out' is a luxury you cannot afford. State your context, state it in specific terms and stick to it.

Useful phrases

This essay will argue that:

- the experience of British rule in India and South Africa encouraged inter-communal violence in both societies, although in distinct ways;

- a comparison of ... and ... shows that the latter is relatively ill equipped and poorly resourced;

- Eyles's comparisons are based on the faulty application of comparative methodology;

- Nayak's work can only be understood in the context of a crisis within late eighteenth-century Russian cultural politics;

- Diamond has not appreciated the current political context that has shaped ....

This form of argument is one of the simplest and most effective. It is also perhaps the easiest type of argument in which to demonstrate originality. Chapter 6 explains how arguments that involve new contexts and new comparisons are within everyone's reach.

Step 2: Summary

When you offer an argument you are making a claim to be providing an analysis. You are not merely describing things but providing an answer to the questions 'How?' and 'Why?'

Be specific about the form your analysis is going to take.

Focus down: cut out all the stuff that isn't helping you to make a clear, understandable case.

Step 3: The one-sentence summary (rough version)

So, what is your argument? In order to make sure that you have one and that it makes sense you need to write it down. And you need to do so in a form that is as concise as possible. This isn't easy: it usually takes several goes. Even then, what you have produced is only the rough version.

If your argument doesn't have a core that can be written in one sentence then it is probably going to be difficult to communicate it clearly to your readership. Later you will need to reformulate (and perhaps expand) this sentence. You will need to produce something polished for your readers. However, what is needed now is something more personal, something rougher. It doesn't matter if it's disjointed or ungrammatical. It doesn't matter if it's written on an old envelope or the back of your hand. All that matters is that you are able to scrawl a line, a thought, that pleases you and captures your basic point.

 **Step 3: Summary**

You've decided on a substantive issue.

You've thought about the form of your argument.

You've written a rough one-sentence summary of it.

Now what?

Now you need to structure your argument. Chapter 2 shows you how to do this.

 Practical tips

Answering the question 'Does it matter?' can be daunting. A simple way to find the answer is by checking out whether the topic you have in mind features in the appropriate journals or other media. If people are talking and writing about it then it is likely to be important.

When choosing an argument it is usually best to keep it simple. Complicated is not the same as sophisticated. Launching into a type of argument you don't really understand often leads to trouble. It is much better to choose ones you are comfortable with and which you can communicate clearly and convincingly.

When choosing a type of argument you do not need to be purist. You can mix and match the six forms introduced in this chapter along with others. The important thing is that you are able to express in clear language the essence of your argument.

You will strengthen your argument if you begin to consider, right from the start, the objections that could be made to it. Your argument will be more convincing if you engage with the most important of these (and they need a place in the structure of your argument).

Exercises: Shorter exercises for groups

1 The winning argument

This exercise should only take 30 minutes or so. It is designed to limber up a group: to get students talking about arguments and thinking about what evidence and reasoning makes them plausible. It has a competitive flavour but is a serious learning experience. A small group (up to five ideally) chooses one topic (everyone needs to be working on the same topic). It should be a topic that anyone can think up an argument about, pretty much off the top of their heads. Each person needs to come up with an argument about the topic (which can then be written in one or two sentences), plus one to three reasons to support their view. Some good topics for this exercise are: Americanisation; religion; environmental protection; ageism; celebrity.

Once everyone has introduced their argument and reasons, the group can have a discussion and decide which argument is the most plausible (and why). In larger sessions, groups of up to five can undertake this exercise among themselves and the winning argument (and its attendant reasons) can be fed into a subsequent round-table discussion and an overall winner chosen.

2 Finding tensions

This is a short exercise (30 minutes) designed to get students in small groups to start thinking about 'big ideas' in terms of argument. The focus is upon finding tensions in well-known and very broad topics (for example: democracy; civilisation; nostalgia; socialism; capitalism). Having chosen one topic each, students need to note down at least one tension within it. At the end of the exercise the group should debate which is the most substantive argument (i.e. which 'tension' appears the most significant). Health warning: this exercise is fairly testing and only works if students have had a preliminary discussion introducing some examples of tension.

3 **Getting started: what is it you really want to say?**

Once begun, arguments have their own dynamic. It is almost as if they start to write themselves. By far the most difficult part of developing an argument is starting it. It can be a depressing time. Such feelings only increase the longer one ponders, the longer one waits for inspiration. The truth is that arguments aren't about waiting but about doing; they emerge from the process of writing.

This exercise is a reminder that your arguments represent you. They are not matters of mere technique but of something much more profound: they communicate to the world your ideas and convictions.

There are four stages to the exercise:

1. Identify an area (a subfield or a topic) within your discipline.

2. Write down two lists of between 10 and 20 short sentences (one-word answers won't do). Do this at speed: take no more than 15 minutes to write down both lists. The first list should consist of opinions and ideas you have about the area in question. It doesn't matter how wild, rough or, for that matter, banal and obvious these items are. What matters is that they reflect views that you actually hold. The second list should consist of opinions and ideas that you believe others have about the area in question but which you yourself disagree with.

3. Go through the lists and circle one sentence from each that strikes you as having potential for the basis of a substantive argument (i.e. the one that is the most interesting, specific, clever, or novel, as opposed to obvious, vague or inconsequential). If you need to circle more than one – because you consider them to be of equal value – that's fine.

4. Finally, compose two short paragraphs defending your choices. What you need to do is explain why you regard the circled items as so special (as a supplementary consideration you should if possible also explain why the other items on your lists are of less consequence and/or are less attractive options).

What you should end up with is a substantive argument that you hold – and would be prepared to defend – and a substantive argument that you do not hold and would be prepared to criticise.

This exercise can be done in groups, with participants swapping their lists at either stage 3 or stage 4 and composing sentences or paragraphs based on each other's work. These should then be read and used as the basis of discussion.

4 The arguments around us

We are surrounded by arguments. They are in our conversation, in the television we watch, in the advertising we see, the work we do. Even such things as landscapes and architecture contain arguments, for they reflect someone's priorities, ideals and analysis. Usually we allow 99.99 per cent of arguments to pass us by. We don't agree or disagree with them but passively allow them to form the framework for our lives. This exercise is about changing that habit, if only for a day. It is about trying to see and hear the arguments that surround us.

All that it requires is a note pad (think of it as your argument diary) and one day of your life. At the end of the exercise you will be trying to sort out the arguments you have gathered into different logical types. However, before this the only division that should interest you is between the different sources of the arguments. Thus you should be entering items under each of the following four categories:

1. Arguments in which you participate (for example, in conversation, polite chat, rows).

2. Arguments that you hear (for example, those that you overhear, hear on TV or the radio, at lectures).

3. Arguments that you see in written form (for example, arguments that you read in books, in advertising, in novels).

4. 'Arguments' that you experience in non-written form (for example, 'arguments' contained in the design of things, people's body language, the planning of things, the structure of one's day). Although such non-verbal signs and symbols do not fit conventional definitions of argument, it is useful to attend to the way things 'speak to you', communicate ideas and opinions, without using words.

Some people find this exercise initially very difficult. The trick is to realise that arguments need identifying, that you need to draw them out, to isolate and name them. Then it becomes a question of knowing when to stop writing. For soon you will find that the world around you is teeming with arguments; that they exist in appalling profusion. When this starts to happen you need to start being selective. Try to write between 15 and 20 items in each of the categories mentioned above. Attempt to make your choices as random as possible. If you are too selective and go only for arguments that interest you, you will probably find that all your items are logically similar.

A diversity of logical forms is useful because the exercise is completed by assigning each of your arguments to one of the six arguments discussed in this chapter, or to a logical argument of your own devising.

Your argument diaries can form the basis of group discussion. They may also be tailored to meet your own particular interests, for example you may decide to look only for arguments about causality, or only arguments that concern issues of gender. It's up to you. However you do it, what you should get out of the exercise is the exciting, if somewhat daunting realisation that not only are you surrounded by arguments but that you have the ability to identify and analyse them.

Further reading

Each of the six arguments discussed in this chapter is recognised and widely used within academic debate. This means that, before employing them yourself, it is necessary to be familiar with the way they have been deployed before, particularly within your own discipline.

The following bibliography is designed to provide a few pointers for those wishing to read more about any of the arguments discussed in this chapter. It is a very limited list. I have not even attempted to provide a comprehensive portrait of the numerous disciplinary introductions to the arguments addressed. The texts mentioned provide either a decent general or disciplinary introduction to a particular argument or an interesting, revealing and research-based instance of their application. The latter are marked with an asterisk.

● Argument 1: Identifying tensions

Tension and contradiction

*Brenkman, J. (2007) *Cultural Contradictions of Democracy: Political Thought Since September 11*. Princeton, Princeton University Press.

*Cooper, F. and Stoler, A. (eds) (1997) *Tensions of Empire, Colonial Cultures in a Bourgeois World*. Berkeley, University of California Press.

*Habermas, J. (1988) *Legitimation Crisis*. Oxford, Polity Press.

Dialectics

Bhaskar, R. (1991) 'Dialectics', in Bottomore, T. (ed.) *A Dictionary of Marxist Thought*. Oxford, Blackwell.

Williams, R. (1983) *Keywords: A Vocabulary of Culture and Society*. London, Fontana.

Deconstruction

Bennington, G. (1993) 'Deconstruction', in Outhwaite, W. and Bottomore, T. (eds) *The Blackwell Dictionary of Twentieth-century Social Thought*. Oxford, Blackwell.

Norris, C. (2002) *Deconstruction, Theory and Practice*. London, Routledge.

● Argument 2: Cause and effect

Qualitative evidence

Texts on qualitative evidence tend to equate the subject with the study of oral and/or personal accounts. For a broader view, which also considers the meaning of events, actions and processes, a good place to look is the literature on historical interpretation.

Creswell, J. (2007) *Qualitative Inquiry and Research Design: Choosing Among Five Approaches: Choosing Among Five Traditions*. London, Sage.

*Henige, D. (2006) *Historical Evidence and Argument*. Madison, University of Wisconsin Press.

Jenkins, K. (1991) *Re-thinking History*. London, Routledge.

Jordanova, L. J. (2000) *History in Practice*. London, Arnold.

Morse, J., Swanson, J. and Kuzel, A. (eds) (2001) *The Nature of Qualitative Evidence*. London, Sage.

Quantitative evidence

Creswell, J. (2002) *Research Design: Qualitative, Quantitative, and Mixed Methods Approaches*. London, Sage.

Fielding, J. and Gilbert, G. (2006) *Understanding Social Statistics*. London, Sage.

Huff, D. (1973) *How to Lie with Statistics*. Harmondsworth, Penguin.

*McClelland, P. (1975) *Causal Explanation and Model Building in History, Economics, and the New Economic History*. Ithaca, Cornell University Press.

Thiessen, V. and Gringrich, P. (1993) *Arguing with Numbers: Statistics for the Social Sciences*. Black Point, Fernwood.

● Argument 3: Starting with observation or starting with an hypothesis

*Achinstein, P. and Hannaway, P. (eds) (1985) *Observation, Experiment, and Hypothesis in Modern Physical Science*. Cambridge, MIT Press.

Chalmers, A. (1999) *What is This Thing Called Science?* Buckingham, Open University.

Gauch, H. (2002) *Scientific Method in Practice*. Cambridge, Cambridge University Press.

Gower, B. (1997) *Scientific Method: A Historical and Philosophical Introduction*. London, Routledge.

Morton, A. (2003) *Philosophy in Practice*. Oxford, Blackwell (chapter 5).

*Popper, K. (2002) *The Logic of Scientific Discovery*. London, Routledge.

● Argument 4: Arguing about words

One of the best sources for the study of language, particularly of etymology, is a good dictionary. The full version of the *Oxford English Dictionary* is a very useful study aid and research tool.

Aitchison, J. (1999) *Linguistics: A New Introduction*. London, Headway.

Cameron, D. (1992) *Researching Language: Issues of Power and Method*. London, Routledge.

Fairclough, N. (2003) *Analysing Discourse: Textual Analysis for Social Research*. London, Routledge.

Nunan, D. (1993) *Introducing Discourse Analysis*. London, Penguin.

*Shapiro, M. (ed.) (1984) *Language and Politics*. Oxford, Blackwell.

Williams, R. (1983) *Keywords: A Vocabulary of Culture and Society*. London, Fontana.

● Argument 5: Contributions and impacts

*Bowser, B. and Hunt, R. (eds) (1996) *Impacts of Racism on White Americans*. Thousand Oaks, Sage Publications.

*Cotton, W. and Pielke, R. (2007) *Human Impacts on Weather and Climate*. Cambridge, Cambridge University Press.

*Frijda, N., Manstead, A. and Bem, S. (eds) (2000) *Emotions and Beliefs: How Feelings Influence Thoughts*. Cambridge, Cambridge University Press.

*Gray, J. (1998) *The Contribution of Educational Research to the Cause of School Improvement*. London, University of London, Institute of Education.

*Segall, M., Campbell, D. and Herskovits, M. (1966) *The Influence of Culture on Visual Perception*. Indianapolis, Bobbs-Merrill Co.

*Smith, M. and Marx, L. (eds) (1994) *Does Technology Drive History? The Dilemma of Technological Determinism*. Cambridge, MIT Press.

● Argument 6: Comparison and context

Bassnett-McGuire, S. (1993) *Comparative Literature*. Oxford, Blackwell.

*Gilmour, R. (1994) *The Victorian Period: The Intellectual and Cultural Context of English Literature, 1830–90*. London, Longman.

*Goertz, G. (1994) *Contexts of International Politics*. New York, Cambridge University Press.

Graham, B. and Nash, C. (2000) *Modern Historical Geographies*. Harlow, Prentice Hall.

*Kachru, Y. and Nelson, C. (2006) *World Englishes in Asian Contexts*. Hong Kong, Hong Kong University Press.

O'Neil, P. (2006) *Essentials of Comparative Politics*. New York, W.W. Norton.

*Sharot, S. (2001) *A Comparative Sociology of World Religions: Virtuosi, Priests, and Popular Religion*. New York, New York University Press.

Sica, A. (ed.) (2006) *Comparative Methods in the Social Sciences*. London, Sage.

2 | Structuring your argument

Putting your ideas in order

It started in your head. Then it became a jumble of notes on the page. Now you have to translate this highly personal tangle of ideas into something comprehensible to the world. You have to communicate your argument. This chapter shows how this can be done, taking you through the **three key steps** you need to take in order to structure your argument. It shows you how to sketch out your ideas in a logical fashion (Step 1). You should then be in a position to write a final one-sentence summary of your argument (Step 2). Finally I offer some guidance on how to work your argument into the different parts of your assignment (Step 3).

Key topics

- Sketching out your argument
- The one-sentence summary
- Putting it all together

Key terms
structure sketching the argument empirical material theory conclusions

At this stage your argument may make perfect sense to you. It may indeed seem utterly precious and beyond all improvement. However, you still have to find a way of explaining it. You have to get it across to people who are reading at speed and who, perhaps, are tired and bored with the effort of marking dozens of scripts. In order to do this you have to learn how to read your own work. Learning how to read your own work involves seeing your efforts through the eyes of a hard-to-convince, heard-it-all-before sceptic. This cantankerous alter ego should be leaning over your shoulder from first draft to final copy. Its presence is especially valuable as you begin to organise your argument, as you give it shape and structure.

In the course of any normal day I find myself involved in a number of arguments. They may take the form of a chat with a friend or shouting at a kitchen utensil (or vice versa). As ordinary, day-to-day events these encounters work fine. Spontaneous, off-the-cuff, and without forethought, they suit their context perfectly well. Academic arguments can't be like that. More to the point, they don't need to be like that because they are **prepared**. If you are given the opportunity to work out an argument, if you have hours, days or weeks to structure it, then it must appear carefully considered and organised.

Students are constantly told to plan their essays, to sketch them out. Without any assistance to develop an intellectual project this mantra can easily appear not only tedious but an attempt to straitjacket the imagination. However, when it is used to enable your intellectual ambitions such advice becomes something liberatory, an essential tool to enable you to get your message, your point of view, across.

Webs and arrows

As the phrase 'sketching an argument' implies, the first stage in communicating your ideas to a wider audience is a graphic one. Literally drawing your argument, representing it through webs, arrows, boxes and so on, is essential because simplification is essential. Picturing your argument demands that you break your ideas down into easily understood and separate parts. It demands that you show the connections between these parts in a straightforward, easy-to-grasp fashion. This act of simplification may sometimes seem to do terrible violence to the baroque details of your original argument. But that is the price of communication. Coherence before complexity.

Everyone has their own style for sketching out an argument. The two most popular methods are **spider diagrams** and **flow diagrams**. Children are often introduced to spider diagrams in school. But whatever your age they are an effective way of generating ideas and seeing the links between them. Spider diagrams start with the question or topic you are going to explore. This goes at the centre of the web. From this point ideas thread outwards, creating a (usually rather lop-sided) web or tree-like structure. Spider diagrams are excellent for the initial, creative stage of your argument. They are not so good in helping you turn all those ideas into a coherent and plausible essay. When written up, the messy fun of the spider's web can collapse into a jumble of unconnected paragraphs. Thus I would recommend that, having done your spider diagram, you move on to something more formal. A structured, flow-diagram method is introduced below. It has four stages.

1. Identify the different parts of your argument

Each of these parts represents a key section of your argument. Identify as few of these as you can get away with. Where appropriate, you may wish to treat these parts as indicating the potential subtitles of your essay. At this stage don't order the parts in any sequence but do give them titles. Again, these titles should be as simple as possible. The example I shall use takes the form of an argument against another author (called Brown) and uses only four basic elements: 'Introduction', 'Counter-evidence', 'Brown's thesis' and 'Conclusion'.

2. Arrange the parts in logical sequence, drawing an arrow between them

The sequence of some of your parts (the introduction, for example) will be obvious. However, you may need to play around with the ordering of the others, testing out whether one really does usefully build on and logically proceed from the other. The most important rule here is a negative one: if part y requires part x to make any sense, then x has to go before y. Generally, arguments should be cumulative, their elements should appear to arise from work already introduced. This isn't an iron rule (and some confident arguers like to flout it) but it is good advice.

3. Unpack the contents of each part

Each of the parts of your essay is like a mini-essay. They should have beginnings, middles and endings. At this stage it is usually appropriate to introduce other key references, theories and positions attached to a name or label that your argument is going to engage. Some people prefer to unpack each part into a sequence of mini-parts, a procedure that makes sure you attend to the logical flow of each section. However, at this micro level, webs can be just as good. Moreover, webs have the advantage of expressing the complexity of linkages (i.e. the way the different parts of your essay connect) and of being more open to creative thought.

4. Draw secondary arrows showing connections between the different parts of your argument

The last phase in sketching your argument is about locating those key links between different parts of your argument that do not appear in the earlier models. You should be making sure that claims made in the introduction are taken up elsewhere and that important new connections that have suddenly struck you are attended to. Now is also a good moment to deal with potential criticism. It is often during this final phase that writers make sure that they have 'dealt with' potential counter-arguments. Ask yourself, 'What other material or causes could be claimed as relevant here?' and 'What objections could be made to this argument?' If you find that these questions make your argument appear untenable then you must abandon it or radically redesign it.

 Step 1: Summary

Identify the different stages of your argument. Sketch them out in sequence, showing the connections between and within each stage.

Keep your sketch as simple as possible.

● Step 2: The one-sentence summary (smooth version)

As you move closer to presenting your argument formally you need to start formulating the particular words and phrases that can communicate your central point. You need to deliver your argument in a way that renders it immediately graspable, in a way that allows readers no excuse for misunderstanding you. At this stage roughly written and personal summaries no longer suffice. In the light of your sketched-out structure you should be able to produce a version of your argument that is coherent, clear and grammatical.

If your essay is not going to be purely theoretical then you will need to include in your one-sentence summary a reference to the empirical evidence you will be drawing on to establish your case. At this stage the so-called **one-sentence summary** can actually be two or even three lines long if necessary. While you don't want a summary that looks like a paragraph, you do want to avoid collapsing your argument into something simplistic. The key is to make your summary as short as your argument will allow. A lot rests on this concise summary. It will be your 'hook-line', something that withstands repetition and to which readers or listeners can easily respond. It is certainly worth taking time with its composition and experimenting with different versions.

 Step 2: Summary

Write a concise summary of your argument. Don't rush it. This is your 'hook-line'.

● Step 3: Putting it all together

If you have completed all the steps outlined so far in this book then actually delivering your argument will be relatively straightforward. You have done the bulk of the intellectual work, you have sorted out your structure and you have encapsulated your core thesis in summary form. All you need to do now is put all this together. In this section I will outline five key things that students should always consider when composing their argument.

If you are writing your essay, rather than presenting it orally, you have the considerable luxury of being able to rework your argument as you deliver it. However, if it is basically sound, I'd advise against adding much supplementary material at this stage. If you have a coherent and interesting line to take then trying to stuff in a load more theses, hypotheses and so on is going to wreck your essay. As Chapter 1 explained, good arguments have a clear and precise focus. To jeopardise that focus is to take a great risk.

Finally, don't forget that arguments arise as a consequence of engaging with debate. This means that references to your source materials need to be woven into your text in the first draft. Sources are not incidentals that can be tacked on at the end. You are writing within a community of scholars. The more clearly you communicate and acknowledge this fact the more informed and sophisticated your work will be judged to be.

The introduction: the most important part of your essay

State your argument clearly and early

The introduction matters. It matters because on any large course (i.e. of over 30 students) you need to make an early impact if your composition is to have a chance of being noticed. It also matters because it is the introduction that establishes your argument. You cannot leave it until the end, nor can you wait for it to dawn on the marker on page 26. You need to get your argument in early (this is true whether your assignment is 20,000 or 500 words). In crude terms, all the material you write after you state your argument is working for you; all the material you write before it is merely preamble.

My personal ideal is for preambles, introductory context and so on not to be longer than one or two paragraphs. The argument should then be stated as a one-sentence summary. And it should be formulated *explicitly* as an argument. Don't allow your readers to miss it. Write something such as 'In this essay it will be argued …'. Remember, where appropriate your summary argument should make reference to the empirical material that you are going to be drawing on.

Make it clear that you are going to engage in debate

The introduction should also be used to tell the reader that your essay is going to engage in debate. In other words you need to indicate that you know an academic literature exists on the subjects you will be addressing and that you are going to 'take sides' or take issue with positions expressed in this debate. Using references, naming authors and/or key texts, and doing so early on in your essay, is nearly always good practice.

State your structure

After stating your argument and indicating the nature of the debate you are engaging, it is usually appropriate to explain the structure of your contribution. This applies to short projects and oral deliveries just as much as it does to long essays. Readers and listeners like to know where they are going. Academic essays are not about the thrill of surprise. Your introduction needs to communicate exactly what is going to be said and how it is going to be evidenced. Being explicit about what you are doing provides less excuse for your markers to write 'poor structure' or 'no clear argument' on their appraisal sheets. It's not imaginative or very sparkling but something like this will do the job for you: 'This essay has three sections. In section one … In section two … Finally, in section three …'.

How to use empirical material

Some students find that once they have mastered argument another problem surfaces. Where once their essays were dominated by 'mere description' now they appear in danger of consisting of 'mere argument'. In other words they feel they don't know how to handle 'evidence', how to 'work it in' to their analysis. This problem is apparent in essays that switch suddenly and awkwardly back and forth from theory to observation, moving clumsily from clearly expressed argument to subsections composed of a jumble of data.

Arguments do not consist simply of introductions and conclusions. They exist to make sense of your facts, to interpret your data. As this implies, your empirical material must be fully introduced at the time you state your argument, i.e. in the introduction. It also means that you need to be constantly returning to the terms and content of your argument while you are considering your empirical material. Your essay is your argument; everything else makes sense because of it. If you find yourself describing things that do not serve a function within your argument and which have no role in your analysis, then you probably need to reassess your direction and start red-lining tangential information.

Although empirical tangents should be avoided it is usually appropriate to treat one's data as complex. More specifically, it is sensible to regard them as diverse and nuanced. Students often make the mistake of homogenising their empirical material, of imagining that it evidences only one point. This leads to meaningless repetition. For example, when using qualitative interview data, pages of quotes are sometimes used to prove the same point again and again. This wastes your data, is very boring to read and gives the impression that you have not 'listened' carefully to your data. After all, it is highly unlikely that such a varied source would repeatedly exemplify exactly the same idea or theme. A more probable and useful outcome is that such data would illustrate different points of emphasis, different reasons to support your overall analysis. This observation could be extended to other kinds of material. Your argument is better served by having it confirmed from a variety of positions than from just one.

Always relate your evidence back to your argument and avoid repetition of evidence.

How to handle theory

Theories are arguments, or, more precisely, theories are arguments recognised as significant and given a name. As this implies, engaging with theory is just another way of saying you are engaging with a known and debated argument. Theory is impossible to avoid. However, this isn't the same thing as saying that you are obliged to place your work within some grand and broadly sketched theoretical context. Indeed it is usually better to be as specific as possible. If one wishes to situate one's work in relation to structuralism, for example, it is better to say what sort of structuralism and whose structuralism than to flatten out that enormously diverse tradition into a series of bland abstractions.

The secret of engaging with theory is not to be found in peppering one's text with 'ologies' and 'isms' or making general half-understood 'big ideas'. Rather it is to be found in being as precise and focused as possible. Here are some 'dos' and 'don'ts' designed to assist you in this task.

Do:

- Flag up your engagement with relevant theory in your introduction. Be particular: refer to specific theories and make reference to named proponents and/or named schools.
- Suggest that you know there are alternative paths within the theory you are engaging.
- Explain why you are using this theory.
- Get some contemporary theoretical references into your essay (to avoid giving the impression that you are 'behind the debate').

How to argue

- Use short sentences. This will help keep your explanations comprehensible.
- Define your theory. It is likely to have different interpretations, so it is important to make yours clear.

Don't:

- Claim too much. It is unlikely that you can refute, or adequately engage with, all the theoretical traditions relevant to your topic. Moreover, unqualified statements such as 'This essay will prove that behaviourism is wrong', or 'This essay will take a postmodern approach' look ignorant. Far better to make more precise claims, such as 'This essay identifies a limitation with behaviourist methodology' or 'This essay applies the techniques of Derridean deconstruction'.

- Use too many theories. One or two theoretical traditions are usually enough. Dragging in more perspectives is going to confuse readers and distract from your main argument. Your essay cannot scan its topic from every angle. Rather it should be offering a specific, useful and self-consciously limited contribution.

- Adopt positions that you don't believe in. It isn't necessary.

- Refer to material that you don't understand. Sometimes you might get away with it but, sooner or later, you'll be found out. It is not a risk worth taking. If you don't understand a theory or area within a theory then avoid writing about it until such time as you do.

● Returning to your argument

In the conclusion or penultimate section of your essay you will need to return explicitly to your central argument. You will also need to say how you have demonstrated and/or proven your central point. As this implies, returning to your argument is not simply a matter of repeating it. At this stage you should be able to discuss it in the light of your evidence and your analysis. It is often appropriate to use this moment to provide an **extended** account of your argument, to flesh out the one-sentence summary of the introduction into a paragraph that can reflect the subtleties of your position. Phrases such as 'This essay has demonstrated that ...', or 'As I have shown in this essay ...' are handy at this point. They remind the reader that the essay has achieved something, that it has fulfilled its initial claims.

Return to your argument towards the end, emphasising what your essay has achieved.

● End with a bang, not a whimper

If you want your essay to have an impact, then your conclusion needs to grab readers' attention. Merely summarising your argument or plodding through a précis of your data is not going to do this. One useful strategy is to rephrase the essay's basic aim in much bolder language. In the conclusion it is often appropriate to articulate your objectives in a punchy, direct fashion (perhaps using personal pronouns and very short sentences). This should be combined with a much more formal explanation. Using both styles can provide a simultaneously stimulating and convincing conclusion to your essay.

Your conclusion should also be used to remind readers of the limitations of your approach. 'This essay has not attempted to ...', or 'The focus of this essay has been limited to ...' are phrases that indicate that you recognise the specificity of your argument. Conclusions can also be used to sketch out the wider implications of your position. This can be done by offering speculative arguments and by suggesting possible new areas of research. Both need to be treated seriously. You must be specific about what kinds of research you have in mind and about why they would be useful. Rather than thinking about your conclusion as a dead end you should imagine it as a room with many open doors. Good conclusions give a sense of possibilities, of the ongoing nature of debate.

Your conclusion needs to reignite the reader's interest in your argument and the wider debate.

 Step 3: Summary

Good arguments have a clear aim and structure. Your argument needs to be sustained throughout your text, both empirically and theoretically. Your conclusion should reiterate your argument and indicate its importance.

Practical tips

Keep it simple. A clear, simple structure allows you to introduce complexity into your account whilst retaining overall coherence. Elaborate structures simply confuse: simple structures allow elaboration.

The need for simplicity and for signposting where you are going is especially important if you are preparing an oral presentation (see Ch 5).

Exercises

1 Practising the sketch, I

Sketching out essay plans is something that one becomes better at with practice. Trying to map out an essay on a topic that you know little about provides some of the best practice of all (because it allows you to focus on the issue of structure without being distracted by content). Below are five arguments. Your task is to sketch them out using the model presented in Step 1 (stages 1 and 2 should suffice).

- The notion of a 'Spanish literary tradition' is a nationalist myth.

- Advanced farming technology is not a sustainable resource within either the developing or developed countries.

- British and French race relations legislation is premised on different conceptions of the reality and desirability of racial demarcation.

- Surrealist novels employ the sexuality of women to represent the content and practice of primitive freedom.

- Modern physics is a product of the Enlightenment but quantum physics is not.

2 Practising the sketch, II

This is a more testing exercise. Again you will need to produce a graphic model of an argument. However, this time there is more information to deal with and your model needs to be correspondingly more complex. You will need to employ stages 1, 2 and 3 (and perhaps 4) of the model presented in Step 1 in order to do justice to the examples.

You can also use these three passages to practise writing one-sentence summaries. Remember, these need to be both concise and informative.

Modern imperialism, it is usually held, intensified the large-scale regional differentiation of the globe .... The colonialism of the Middle Ages was quite different. When Anglo–Normans settled in Ireland or Germans in Pomerania or Castilians in Andalusia, they were not engaged in the creation of a pattern of regional subordination. What they were doing was reproducing units similar to those in their homelands. The towns, churches and estates they established simply replicated the social framework they knew from back home. The net result of this colonialism was not the creation of 'colonies', in the sense of dependencies, but the spread, by a kind of cellular multiplication, of the cultural and social forms found in the Latin Christian core. The new lands were closely integrated with the old. Travellers in the later Middle Ages going from Magdeburg to Berlin and on to Wroclaw, or from Burgos to Toledo and on to Seville, would not be aware of crossing any decisive social or cultural frontier.

(Robert Bartlett, *The Making of Europe: Conquest, Colonization and Cultural Change 950–1350*, 1993)

One of the greatest enemies of science is pseudo-science. In a scientific age, prejudice and passion seek to clothe themselves in a garb of scientific respectability; and when they cannot find support from true science, they invent a pseudo-science to justify themselves. We all know that the Devil can quote Scripture for his own purpose: today we are finding that he can even invent a false Scripture from which to quote.

Nowhere is this lamentable state of affairs more pronounced than in regard to 'race'. A vast pseudo-science of 'racial biology' has been erected which serves to justify political ambitions, economic ends, social grudges, class prejudices.

(Julian Huxley and A. C. Haddon, *We Europeans: A Survey of 'Racial' Problems*, 1935)

Revenge is a kind of wild justice; which the more man's nature runs to, the more ought law to weed it out. For as for the first wrong, it doth but offend the law; but the revenge of that wrong, putteth the law out of office. Certainly, in taking revenge, a man is but even with his enemy; but in passing it over, he is superior: for it is a prince's part to pardon. And Solomon, I am sure, saith, It is the glory of a man to pass by an offence. That which is past, is gone, and irrevocable; and wise men have enough to do, with things present, and to come: therefore, they do but trifle with themselves, that labour in past matters.

(Francis Bacon, *The Essays*, 1985; originally published 1625)

3 Evidence and argument

It is important to integrate your evidence into your argument. A useful way of thinking about this issue is to pay attention to the way people in the media, such as journalists, employ their facts. The exercise that follows is a very simple but often highly revealing way of interrogating this relationship.

First of all you need to choose a newspaper article or television presentation (the latter will need to be taped). Try and pick something that is short yet appears to be addressing substantive issues (this makes the exercise easier). The exercise has three stages:

1. Your initial act of analysis is to note down the basic, overall argument that is being put forward. As always you should try and express this in as concise yet informative terms as possible.

2. Then write down *all* the evidence that is being offered by the news source in question to support this argument, however slight.

3. The next step is to arrange this information into five columns: 'proves' (i.e. no more evidence is required), 'strongly supports' (i.e. offers substantial support but not proof of the argument), 'weakly supports' and 'irrelevant'. Where evidence is merely being repeated then it should be noted in both one of the four preceding columns and the fifth column, which can be labelled 'repeats'.

Although this exercise can be completed by one person it is also effective when conducted by a group (with all participants using the same piece of journalism). Having completed the exercise, each member of the group should then identify what they consider to be a key or illuminating piece of information from the first, second and fourth columns (i.e. 'proves', 'strongly supports' and 'irrelevant').

These items can then be compared and used as the basis of a discussion on the relationship between evidence and argument within the group. Evidence from the other columns is useful to supplement these discussions.

3

Arguments for all occasions

Different assignments require different approaches

This chapter explains the role of argument in dissertations, essays, exams, group work, grant applications and 'pitches'. As we shall see, the plausibility of an argument is, in part, determined by how well it has been adapted to fit particular situations. The differences between the style of argument expected in the social sciences, humanities and sciences are briefly surveyed at the end of the chapter.

Key topics
- Different stages
- Different tasks (dissertations, essays, exams, group work, grant applications and pitches)
- Different disciplinary traditions

Key terms
expectations   assessments   adapting your argument

● Expectations at different stages

Distinctions are often made between what is *expected* of students at different stages. A first-year student is not *expected* to be offering arguments that are as innovative, sophisticated or as well sourced as a student in their final year. The higher up you go on the academic ladder the more emphasis is placed on argument. By the time you are doing a doctorate (a PhD) you are supposed to be able to support an original and substantive argument of book length. But is it helpful to worry about **expectations**? If you are using them to push you towards producing work that is ambitious and rigorous then they are serving a purpose. If, by contrast, you are using them as an excuse – to imagine that because you are a first year you don't need to bother working up an argument – then they are holding you back. First-year students aren't marked down for offering substantive, original arguments. Quite the opposite. It may not be *expected* but it is, nevertheless, always something to be hoped for. The point is, never use stage expectations to *limit* yourself.

● Arguments for different tasks

Sustaining a convincing argument is the central performance of intellectual life. Those types of assessment that do not need an argument are the least demanding and least rewarding. Multiple-choice exams and portfolios of notes may be inevitable in an age of vast class sizes. But they are the zombies of academic assessment: hollowed out of creativity and lifeless. The life-blood of education is the freedom given to students to pursue an argument. For many students the centrepiece of their entire course is a long project (often called a dissertation) researched and devised largely by themselves. It is in this long essay that learning how to argue really comes into its own.

Dissertations

There is no hiding. The dissertation is an exposed place. You have to write 5,000, 10,000, 20,000 words, maybe many more. And the central issue, the thing that is being proposed and tested, is your ability to offer and develop a plausible argument that weaves together all those thousands of words. *This isn't easy.* It's hard work. It will involve false starts, copy screwed up and tossed in the bin, several drafts. If this is happening it's a good sign: it's what all writers and researchers have to go through. Nevertheless, you can make life easier for yourself by thinking about the role of argument in the dissertation. Below I offer some tips to help you on your way.

What's your centrepiece?

It is usual for dissertations to have one or two central arguments that bond the whole together. A number of subsidiary arguments may also be set out, both in the introduction and along the way.

Tell us why it matters

In most cases it is a good idea either to precede or follow up your main argument with a statement that explains why this topic and/or argument matter (why they are important and to whom).

Each chapter or part needs to fit into the argument

Each chapter or part needs to have an introduction, which sets out its relationship to the central argument. Usually this means telling the reader how the chapter or part is contributing to, or engaging with, the development of the main argument. This does *not* mean repeating word for word the argument offered in the introduction to the dissertation. The dissertation should appear to be **moving forward** with each new chapter.

For example, your main argument is that something (let's call it *x*) is contradictory. In the introduction to Chapter 3 (let's title it 'The Role of *z*') you write: 'In order to understand the contradictions of *x* we need to examine them in relation to *z*'.

Some chapters are more 'stand alone' than others. This is especially true in longer and postgraduate dissertations and where chapters are dealing with a distinct requirement of the assignment (for example, that it has to have a separate chapter on methodology). However, these chapters still need an argument, set out at their start (and, sometimes, in the introduction to the whole dissertation as well). Methodology chapters require an argument explaining your choice of method. For example: 'Research into *x* has been dominated by method *y*. In this chapter I introduce and explain the necessity for a revised version of method *y*'.

Signposting

Signposts are the visible structure of your dissertation and argument. Aside from the contents page and introduction (see pages 46–7) there are five main opportunities for signposting:

- The titles of chapters and subheadings can be used to help readers see the development of your argument.
- It is useful for chapters to have an introduction that explains their role in the overall argument.
- Chapters can benefit from conclusions that summarise the main points and remind readers how they fit in with the overall argument.

- At the end of each chapter it can be useful to add a line or two explaining how the chapter leads to the next.
- The conclusion to the whole dissertation needs to come back to the overall argument, rephrasing and re-imagining it in the light of evidence presented in the dissertation (*not* simply repeating it).

Writing without chapters or headings

If you are not allowed or don't want to use chapters or other subheadings you still need to produce a coherent and cumulative piece of work. By using paragraph breaks to structure the text you can employ all the points mentioned above. Signpost phrases, such as 'I shall now turn to ...' or 'Before addressing *x* we need to examine *y*', are helpful ways of guiding readers through the text.

Things to avoid

All 'evidence of reading': no argument

Students are reminded, often and remorselessly, that they need to show evidence of reading. One unfortunate consequence is that some take this to mean that they should crowd as many references on to each page as physically possible. The end product often looks like a randomly generated list of authors and summaries. Although the 'coverage' of the field may be great, the argument has been lost. This is often a problem associated with so-called 'literature review' chapters. In fact the phrase 'literature review' can be misleading. Just outlining a bunch of relevant articles is an exercise in mere description. In 'literature review' chapters it is recommended that you:

- set out in the introduction of the chapter that you are going to draw on a few key references in order to show how the literature in your field is dominated or characterised by a particular type of work or argument;
- put in other, supporting, references along the way, using phrases such as, 'By contrast, Davies shows us that ...' or 'This position is also supported by Patel in her ...'.

Bullet points

Generally speaking, bullet points should be used very sparingly, if at all. For greater clarity, it is sometimes permissible (especially in the social sciences) to set out your arguments bullet-point style in the introduction of a dissertation (but do check with your supervisor).

Signpost overload

A plethora of subheadings, repeating your argument often and at length, or spending anything more than a sentence or two summarising or flagging up what the next chapter will bring, are all things to avoid. The opportunity to signpost should not always be taken: too many can ruin a good dissertation.

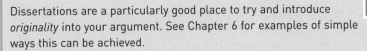

Dissertations are a particularly good place to try and introduce *originality* into your argument. See Chapter 6 for examples of simple ways this can be achieved.

Essays

Shorter assignments work best if the author sticks to one or two central arguments. At the same time authors need to communicate their knowledge of the wider field and the debates that are animating it. The ideal is to make the reader know you are aware of the diversity of relevant issues but also have a clear idea of what should be given priority and why.

We can understand better the place of argument in essays by looking at a set question. These are often very 'open' in form. You could answer them correctly with a laundry list of events and names (and get a low mark). You can also apply a focused argument to them (and get a higher mark). For the latter you need to provide an initial statement that establishes both your coverage and knowledge of the field and your ability to offer a clear argument.

Q: What led to the Plum crisis of 1905?

A: The 1905 Plum crisis was provoked by a variety of interconnected factors, including the decline of custard production and the rise of mail-order shopping. However, its principal cause and context was the increasing political power of the agricultural trade unions.

This kind of statement sets out your argument and other relevant material. It is a balance that should be maintained throughout the essay. The precise weighting of the balance depends on the question. As we shall see in the next section, sometimes you need more emphasis on the argument, sometimes on the wider context.

Exam questions

The key word in a question is the 'instruction verb', the verb that tells you to 'describe', 'analyse', 'compare' and so on. One of the functions of this verb is to let you know about the role of argument in your answer. There are three kinds of exam question:

- those that do not ask for argument;
- those where argument is required;
- those where argument takes the lead.

Questions where argument is unnecessary

Sometimes students are simply being asked to relay data or to show the accuracy of their grasp of a body of information. Such questions do not require evidence of analysis. Examples include: *list, enumerate, summarise, draw a diagram*.

Questions where argument is required

These questions place equal or even more weight on your ability to convey a range of accurate information than they do on your skills as an arguer. As a consequence unprepared students overlook the opportunity they offer to develop an argument. But it is an opportunity that good students will not miss. Examples include: *define, describe, compare, contrast*.

- **Define:** This is a great opportunity to impress. After all, there is invariably more than one way of defining something and an argument to be made about what constitutes the most useful definition. Where possible, draw on academic sources to show that there is a debate about the best definition.

  Q: Define fruit fetishism.

  A: Conventional definitions of fruit fetishism emphasise dessert fruits (for example, Legume, 2006). However, recent years have witnessed a new focus on the ambivalent place of the seeded 'vegetable' ....

- **Outline/describe:** An answer that merely relays a set of facts might pass but it is unlikely to get great marks. When you are being asked to sort out information (and not simply list it) then you need an argument about priority, an argument that distinguishes what is central and what is tangential. This is true of all *outline* and *describe* questions.

Q: Outline the 1968 Rhubarb Conspiracy Act.

A: The main feature of the Rhubarb Conspiracy Act was the making unlawful of trades union activity in the industry. Other aspects of the Act, such as those that applied to soft fruit producers, were already regulated under previous legislation ....

- **To what extent:** This phrase demands an argument about extent: in other words, about the range, reach and importance of something.

- **In what ways:** This requires an argument that introduces and orders, and perhaps explains, the variety of something.

- **Trace:** Here argument needs to be about the development of something; usually you are being asked to describe the emergence or change in the nature of something over a period of time.

- **Demonstrate:** The argument needs to focus upon showing or proving something.

- **Compare:** The argument should be about what is similar or the same and what is different between two or more things.

- **Contrast:** This is like compare, but with an emphasis on what is different between two or more things (also *distinguish*, where the emphasis is entirely on differences).

- **Relate:** Here you need to show the connections between two or more things.

- **Review:** This requires an argument that offers or emerges from an overview of something.

Questions where argument takes the lead

When you are asked to *explain*, *discuss*, *consider*, *assess* or *critically analyse* something, you are being asked to assert an argument. Questions like this – which offer open-ended invitations for you to explore a topic – are looking for answers where argument takes the lead. Thus these are questions where the balance between covering relevant information and argument creaks towards the latter.

- **Discuss:** Many exam questions will ask you to discuss a topic.

    Q: Discuss the global collapse of mozzarella consumption. [The desire just to fill the page up with everything you know about the topic is strong. But don't. Hang your essay on one or two main arguments.]

A: In this essay it will be argued that the decline of mozzarella consumption is attributable to two principal factors: the decline in quality of the product and the decay of the distribution network.

Of course you will go on to discuss other factors, but by leading on a clear argument you're giving yourself a much better chance of a decent overall mark.

- **Critically … :** This adverb is often applied to 'question verbs' ('critically analyse'; 'critically assess' and so on). It is not a request to say a lot of rude things about something. But it does carry the implication that you should be offering an argument that is, in some way, challenging received wisdom. One of the ways to do this is to flag up a dominant or conventional way of approaching the subject and then introduce an alternative.

Q: Critically explore the cultural significance of Cheddar cheese in England.

A: Cheddar has long been considered by social historians a key metonym of English nationhood (see de Board, 2008). However, drawing on the recent work of Grater, this essay will argue that over the past 20 years Cheddar has come to signify the globalisation and, hence, dispersal of ideas of national identity.

- **Evaluate:** This requires an assessment of different aspects or viewpoints of a phenomenon. It will often include consideration of advantages and disadvantages but be careful that your argument is not smothered by a 'list-based' approach to either.

- **Analyse:** Analysis is the examination and identification of constituent parts. Arguments that offer analysis require an explanation of what constitutes and causes something.

- **Justify/defend/support:** These all require an argument asserting the case for something. Such arguments are made more plausible where they engage and carefully refute (using the most moderate of language) counter-argument and counter-evidence.

Rescuing lost arguments

The argument was there … and then it just kind of wandered off, leaving you hemmed in by a jungle of verbiage. It is a common exam scenario. It starts well, the argument is in place and then, about a page or two in, you realise that you are rambling without purpose or direction. And in exams there is no way back, apart from crossing out previous text (which is time-consuming and messy). But arguments are usefully flexible. They can work *ex post facto* (telling us about what went on before) as well as predictively (telling us what will happen next). Indeed, if you have merely strayed off the point (cf. been misleading or inaccurate) then, occasionally, getting lost can be a good thing. It makes you pause and pull the material you have just written into the argument and clarifies the course that the essay is now going to take. At such times, a 'rescue' phrase is useful, for example:

> Although overlooked by Davies and Patel, the issue of [whatever you have just been writing about] is a significant aspect of [state connection to terms of the question and/or your initial argument]. In the remainder of the essay I return to [your initial argument and/or evidence].

Having one or two key references (named authorities) that can be linked to simple, one-sentence arguments will help give your exam essay intellectual punch. Your own argument will be strengthened by being introduced alongside (whether in support of or as a critique of) other arguments.

Group work

Isn't group work fun? There's nothing quite like falling out with people you barely know over something you barely understand .... Well, that's how it can feel when you're trying to introduce argument into the proceedings. The argument is often the place where group work comes unstuck. This is usually for one of two reasons:

- The group members each contribute distinct parts, which are then cobbled together with insufficient attention to weaving them into a coherent and overall argument.
- The principle of lowest common denominator kicks in. Rather than working up a substantive argument the group members each privately decide it is far easier to go with an idea that is banal enough to be mutually unobjectionable.

The first problem is easily overcome with enough co-ordination. However the initial division of labour is structured it is usually a good idea to have *each* member of the group take a critical look at the whole draft. Thus, although there may be one principal co-ordinator, the responsibility for pulling the project together and ironing out tensions in the argument is shared.

The second problem results from a misunderstanding. Group work is not about finding out what a group of people can all agree on. It isn't a peace conference between warring parties. It is more akin to a group of actors working up a performance. The end result needs to be a useful academic intervention. The first thing a group needs to do is brainstorm for some interesting, rigorous and creative ideas. The idea with the best potential should then be developed, irrespective of individual beliefs and prejudices. In individual work this kind of trade-off between what you believe and what you write isn't usually necessary, but in group work it is.

> ✔ During their initial meetings groups should set themselves the challenge of coming up with a substantive and interesting argument. This argument will be the key to the success of the assignment so it is best to begin developing it as soon as possible.

Grant applications

A grant bid is an argument that a **proposed activity** is so necessary, timely, well-conceived and exciting that it requires funding. Hence, the bid needs to show that a project should and can be done and the grant writers know how to do it. Projects that are over-ambitious and which are vague as to method, timescale and outcome, are unlikely to get any cash. Grant writing also demands an attention to the convictions of the potential donor: your bid has to fit into their expectations and assumptions.

Grant bids demand formal, 'official sounding' language and a clear structure. Bullet points and charts showing the precise division of labour, the precise use of funds and a week-by-week schedule give an impression that a grant will be spent wisely and well. Grant bids require a statement of context or background that introduces the current state of knowledge or activity in the field. This summary needs to be tailored in such a way that the reader sees the need for the proposed project. This statement is usually followed by a project outline which provides answers to the following questions: 'What is the project?'; 'Who will benefit from it?'; 'How is it going to be done?'

Pitches

Pitches should not be confused with academic oral presentations (discussed in Chapter 5). Pitching is about trying to convince an audience to buy your idea (sometimes literally). The cliché of pitching makes it appear dependent on off-the-wall ideas and an artificial smile. However, it is almost certainly a mistake to imagine that style is more important than substance and that windy generalities are more convincing than specific information. A good pitch requires forethought and research, especially since it is often followed up by questions. It is useful to work your pitch up in three versions: the one-sentence version, the three-sentence version and the long or full version. The shorter versions can be deployed at the start and the end of your pitch and to field questions. However, the main audience for the shorter versions is you: they make sure you have a focused and clear key argument.

Many pitches have a three-part structure:

- **Context:** The need/demand for [whatever it is you are pitching] is outlined.
- **Solution:** [Whatever it is you are pitching] is outlined as a solution.
- **Practicality:** [Whatever it is you are pitching] is outlined as a 'do-able', practical proposal.

Throughout, try to use specific examples and concrete and up-to-date information. By the end of the pitch your audience should be thinking: 'Why aren't we doing/making this already?'

● Different disciplinary traditions

The importance of argument transcends disciplines. However, it remains the case that different disciplinary areas have developed somewhat different 'cultures of argument'. I provide a few brief tips below. The soundest advice though is to look at the place of argument within your own specific field. Also, if you are taking a course led by someone who has published their academic work (or, failing this, clearly admires somebody else's) then read some of it. There is no better way of finding out what they think is a good argument.

Academia can be split into three broad areas: the social sciences, the humanities and the sciences.

The social sciences

(For example, sociology, economics, business studies, education, politics, psychology, human geography.)

As the name implies the social sciences are influenced by a scientific model of intellectual enquiry. What this means in practice is that considerable attention is paid to the clarity and rational build-up of arguments and the reliability and sourcing of evidence. Clear statements of what your argument is, the structure of your argument and a well-signposted route through it tend to be appreciated and rewarded. Although there has been a move towards less staid and more polemical approaches in some areas of the social sciences, the dominant tradition is still to look at texts as tools that should be judged according to their clarity and the utility of their structure and aim.

The humanities

(For example, English, history, philosophy, modern languages, classics, fine art.)

The social sciences and humanities share the same basic regard and approach to argument. However, a couple of distinctive points of emphasis can be identified. First, arguments in the humanities need to work harder to be integrated into a confident, satisfying – one might say elegant – form. Bullet points, a clutter of subheadings, tedious repetition of phrases such as 'it shall be argued', can strike readers in the humanities as clumsy and symptomatic of intellectual dullness. Hence, a narrative style is favoured, in which arguments are central but greater freedom is accorded to students to be engaging and intellectually expansive (i.e. to roam not off the point but around it). Second, the more scientific forms of argument, notably hypothesis testing and quantitative techniques, while not unknown in the humanities, are not common.

The sciences

Students in the pure sciences (physics and chemistry) will have little use for many of the forms of argument introduced in this book. These sciences are founded upon theory and experiment that directly address the most basic units of nature. The resultant argument usually takes the form of demonstrating, in as succinct a fashion as possible, a causal chain of events. This chain of events is often understood to derive from hypothesis testing and/or allied to arguments about cause and effect and comparison. In the applied sciences (which include agriculture, engineering, ITC, environmental science and biology), a similar range of argument is apparent but there is greater scope to develop them into essay-style, narrative explanations.

Mathematicians use an abstract form of the cause and effect argument (maths can be understood as a pure science, where the basic unit of nature is logic). It is perhaps the single area of intellectual life where it is appropriate to claim an argument offers complete proof (see '**QED**' in the Glossary).

 ## Practical tips

Arguments need to be evidenced. Your argument will be more convincing if you make it clear what your evidence is right from the start. The simplest way to do this is by use of the phrase 'Drawing on ...'. For example, 'Drawing on census data from 2001, this essay will argue ...'.

To avoid readers getting the impression you are drifting from the title of your assignment, or the terms of the exam question that has been set try to a) make use of the terms contained in the title (or exam question) in your key one-sentence summary and b) offer definitions of one or two of the key terms in the title (or exam question) early on in your assignment.

 ## Exercises

1 Thinking about exam questions

This exercise is designed to get students to think about the different forms and expectations of exam questions. Before doing it, remind yourself that a good answer will contain an argument. The exercise works well when it is based on questions about things which we all think we know about. This also means that in tutorial or seminar situations the deliberately general topics offered below could be replaced by more discipline-specific ideas. In a group situation this exercise can be undertaken by way of a few notes, or a paragraph, written by each participant. This can then be read out, compared and discussed.

Choose any one topic from the following:

love; nostalgia; genius; democracy; anxiety

Now apply any two of the following questions to your chosen topic:

discuss it; describe it; define it; justify it; critically analyse it; evaluate it

2 Pitching ideas

Pitching isn't that common in academia but it is a lively way of getting students to develop and defend arguments. In this exercise, you are asked to choose an idea from the following list (again these could be replaced by more discipline-specific ideas):

world government; euthanasia; compulsory religious observance; compulsory atheism; vegetarianism.

Participants need to write up a one-sentence version and a long or full version (which can be as short as three minutes). The exercise can be followed up with a discussion of which pitch was the most convincing and/or compelling. The full pitch needs to contain:

(a) context: in which the need/demand for [whatever it is you are pitching] is outlined;

(b) solution: [whatever it is you are pitching] is outlined as a solution;

(c) practicality: [whatever it is you are pitching] is outlined as a 'do-able', practical proposal.

4

How to criticise arguments

Key terms for critical engagement

Critique is an essential component of good argument. This chapter introduces seven key terms that will help you develop and express your critical skills.

Key topics
- The art of constructive criticism
- Key terms for criticising arguments

Key terms
critique constructive engagement criticism

I said at the beginning of this book that good argument is about advancing knowledge rather than winning. However, this isn't the same thing as saying that a good argument shouldn't contain criticism. Far from it. Without criticism, debate stops. It is the nature and form of criticism that matters. If it is intellectually honest and rigorous, ready to admit mistakes, a refutation of self-serving sophistry, then it serves the cause of academic argument. It is in this spirit that this chapter introduces some essential critical terms and explains how to use them.

The forms of criticism that I introduce here are supplementary to those addressed in Chapter 1. In the earlier chapter straightforward refutations were mentioned – terms such as 'mistaken' and 'wrong' – as well as more subtle ideas, such as 'contradictory' and 'incoherent'. The concepts that are covered in this chapter are of this subtler variety. They tend to imply not that an argument is necessarily all wrong but rather that it is, in a specific and identifiable sense, limited and inadequate.

Students often find it difficult to decide just how damning their criticisms should be. A common mistake is to inflate the scale and implications of one's critique; to take a decent idea and push it to extremes. It is an error that transforms one's efforts from something constructive and useful into something scurrilous. It is important to remember that academic arguments are not designed to destroy everything they come into contact with. If you want to be the mighty victor in a devastated landscape there are (unfortunately) plenty of other arenas that will accommodate your megalomania. In higher education, criticism only convinces when it is adding to a debate, when it is building, not demolishing. This also implies that, where the possibility arises that your criticism may be misconstrued as having more targets than you intended, then it is appropriate to state not merely what you *are* criticising, but what you are not. Short 'let-out' clauses are often sufficient for this purpose. For example: 'Although Sivanandan's central thesis is now widely accepted, her particular interpretation of … remains problematic', or 'It is not my intention in this essay to criticise the current application or practice of the Institute's work, only its structure and organisation'.

● Simplistic

Saying something is simplistic is easy. It is also often accurate. The difficulty lies in supporting such a charge. This is not as straightforward as it can sometimes appear. For 'simplistic' is not the same as 'simplifying'. The latter is a necessary aid to understanding. We need to simplify things, to focus on certain aspects and not others, in order to create form and structure in our material. We must simplify in order to comprehend. The problem comes when either:

- this process is taken too far and vital context and information is lost;
- people are ignorant of the existence of important complicating factors; or
- analysts believe that the final cause or essence of a phenomenon can be located in one particular thing when, in fact, it cannot.

When one encounters arguments marred by any of these attributes it is appropriate to criticise them as simplistic. The last example mentioned may also be called reductionist, a term discussed in the section below.

Many of the cultural and scientific ideas that surround us could be called simplistic. The very ubiquity of the phenomenon means that it is not a charge that is likely to excite readers. No one is going to fall off their stool because you have claimed that, for example, contemporary accounts of evolution are simplistic. A more likely reaction is a bored grunt of recognition. Arguments based on this form of criticism need to work hard to ensure a more positive response. More specifically, they have to make the precision and utility of their central charge plain. Indeed, such arguments only really come alive if they are able to explain the causes and consequences of the act of over-simplification under scrutiny. What was it that made it possible? Is it consistent? Why does it matter? These are the types of question you need to ask if you are to make this type of criticism intellectually illuminating and interesting. They will also prevent you from being hoist with your own petard. After all, to offer 'simplistic' as a general accusation is not only mundane but, in all likelihood, an instance of over-simplification.

● Reductionism and determinism

Many of the 'boo' words in intellectual debate actually describe things that, at some level, are inevitable and necessary. As noted above, simplifying is essential if one's material is to be understood. Claiming that the cause of a complex array of processes is to be found within one very specific thing is not necessarily illegitimate. Only if this claim is misleading may it be accused of being simplistic. Another word is also appropriate for this particular practice – reductionism.

The charge of reductionism is an important critical tool because so many of the influential theories of our day, in both academic and popular discourse, claim to have discovered or otherwise sourced the root cause of social and natural processes. For example, Marxists claim that the real causes of social change lie in the economic distinction and conflict between those who produce and those who accumulate profit. Many sociobiologists are equally convinced that the explanation for social behaviour may be found in human evolution. Both of these examples are highly developed theories that make an explicit claim to have located and understood the real cause of things. Thus, to charge them with reductionism (more specifically, one might charge Marxism with class or economic reductionism and sociobiology with biological or genetic reductionism) necessitates an ability to dispute their central claims. It also requires that we can evidence or postulate a more diverse set of causes than they themselves consider. As this implies, reductionism is not a term that should be used lazily. It demands careful thought on the part of the accuser. It is especially important to identify exactly what is misleading and incomplete about the 'reduction' one is attempting to tackle.

The charge of reductionism can also be deployed against those who, while not advancing any recognised reductionist theory, structure their argument in such a way as to suggest mistakenly and simplistically that one particular thing is the cause or root of many other things. Let's take an example. Imagine you are confronted with an historical explanation of the location of Italian seaports that provides no serious analysis of any contributing factor other than these ports' proximity to a major city. This is clearly an example of over-simplification. But we can be more precise than this: it is an argument that reduces its material to one particular cause. We may say, therefore, that its claim to have uncovered the key component influencing seaport location evidences not a clarity of focus but a narrowness of intellectual grasp, a paucity of imagination. Again it is important to stress that simplifying material, even reducing it down to one or more core factors, is not in itself objectionable. It is when this process results in misleading and misinformed analysis that it becomes problematic. It is for this reason alone that the term reductionist is employed as a term of criticism.

'Reductionism' and 'determinism' are often used interchangeably. However, they do not mean the same thing. A determinist is someone who believes that for everything that occurs there are conditions such that, given them, nothing else could have occurred. In this sense determinists seem to be suggesting that everything is **predetermined** – that whatever does happen was bound to happen. This conviction encourages circular argument. However, criticisms of determinism can also have another, more general, target in mind. For determinism is often equated with the broader error of representing complex processes through crude and formulaic models of causation. Thus the term has also come to denote overly mechanical, rigid and crude explanations of social or natural change.

Reductionism is one of the most useful terms for those wishing to build an argument based on critique. It is easily grasped as an idea and when deployed carefully combines clarity with sophistication.

● Bias

To have a bias is to have a specific and prior disposition, or prejudice, in favour of certain interpretations of events and against others. To accuse someone of bias means that you believe this disposition is mistaken and/or unfair. It also implies that you think they should be unbiased or disclose their prejudices. The more general and imprecise this criticism is, the less useful and convincing it becomes. Indeed, in many areas of academic debate, a general charge of bias is inappropriate. For example, what would it mean to criticise a political philosophy, such as conservatism or anarchism, of bias? The advocates of particular political programmes always have allegiances and traditions. Against this background the idea that there exists a non-biased, objective, value-free, 'scientific' politics is highly dubious.

By and large students engaged in interpreting social and historical narratives would be well advised to avoid making sweeping accusations of bias. The idea of bias only becomes useful when it is translated into a much more specific criticism or when it is being applied in an area where the notion that there exist non-biased approaches is widely accepted. Examples of the former include the claim that a piece of work is Eurocentric (in other words that it presents a blinkered, European-based perspective) or androcentric (in other words that it presents a blinkered, male-based perspective). Such terms suggest an ability to identify a specific prejudice and to show how it affects the judgements made within one's material. Although these specific criticisms imply the possibility of more informed and less biased perspectives, they do not necessarily lead to, or involve, a claim of objectivity.

If you are working within an area where being neutral and 'value free' is an integral part of the prevailing methodological tradition, then the charge of bias can be employed more straightforwardly. This is particularly apparent within the natural sciences; for example, almost the entire field of racial science was scientifically discredited from the 1910s onwards by scientists and anthropologists who explained the inadequacy and inconsistency of the data on supposed racial difference by reference to bias. Racial science, it was widely concluded, was bad science. Accusations of bias within the natural sciences, as well as within those areas of the social sciences and history that claim to be scientific, can be highly revealing.

> ✓ The difficult thing is not making an accusation of bias but to show how and explain why particular manifestations of bias have particular, identifiable impacts. It is the causes and nature of bias that are of interest, its workings and impacts. General or blanket condemnations act to obscure these specificities.

● Circularity

> The existence of a personal God is proved by the Bible; and the authority of the Bible must, of course, be accepted because it was inspired by God.
>
> (Mander, 1936)

There is something wrong with this argument. It is an example of circular logic. The first claim is proved by reference to a second claim that depends on the acceptance of the first claim. Circular statements make weak arguments. Spotting and explaining them can provide students with insightful and important interventions in ongoing debates. Unfortunately, most forms of circularity are not nearly as obvious as the example given above. They tend to be hidden by a multitude of facts and tangents. As this suggests, the skill in identifying circularity usually relies on an ability to separate 'the circular bit' from the rest.

It is often useful to define the specific place where, and the specific conditions under which, one finds circularity within an argument. This point is easier to appreciate by looking at an example:

If Sokal retains the definition of technology she advanced in *The New Lords of Science*, as 'the essence of civilisation', then her subsequent thesis that civilisation has been most significantly advanced by technological innovation becomes circular.

By making it clear under what conditions circularity can be identified and thus placing clear limits on the scope and aim of their argument, the author of this passage provides a constructive intervention. Unless one is feeling particularly confident, making huge and general accusations of circularity (for example, implying that every aspect of one's subject's work is circular) are best avoided. This advice also reflects the fact that, when you start looking, it soon becomes apparent that circularity is incredibly common. This shouldn't put you off criticising work where circularity is a problem; but it does reinforce the point that the more focused and clear one's identification of the circularity one is addressing, the more impressive and helpful one's criticism will be.

● Teleology

Teleology is often called 'the design argument'. It is a form of explanation based on a claim to have deciphered some ultimate overarching plan or structure (*telos* is a Greek word meaning 'purpose' or 'end'). The concept can most easily be grasped in its theological sense. Within monotheistic religions teleology refers to the doctrine that every aspect of the material world can be explained by reference to God's plan: that everything from the shape of seahorses' tails to bubonic plague has a purpose and a function within His overarching vision.

Teleology requires considerable faith in the capacity and the accuracy of people's ability to identify the nature of this ultimate design or designer. However, despite the apparent grandiosity of this claim, far from being restricted to a theological backwater, teleology became a powerful current within natural and social science. Indeed, in the nineteenth century naturalist and theological teleologies were sometimes difficult to tell apart. Consider, for example, Maury's (1874) account of the function of the oceans in his *The Physical Geography of the Sea*:

The sea, therefore, we infer, has its offices and duties to perform; so, may we infer, have its currents, and so, too, its inhabitants; consequently, he who undertakes to study its phenomena, must cease to regard it as a waste of waters. He must look upon it as a part of the exquisite machinery by which the harmonies of nature are preserved, and then he will begin to perceive the developments of order and evidences of design which make it a most beautiful and interesting subject for contemplation.

Although teleology has fallen from favour in many areas of science, one sphere where it has continued to provide an important paradigm is within explanations of animal and human behaviour. When we explain such behaviours in terms of their utility within a process of species competition and evolution or, more simply, in terms of their role in obtaining the goal of individual survival, we are explaining them in terms of an end that defines the means. As this implies, much contemporary evolutionary biology and sociobiology is teleological; it offers a modern version of the 'design argument'.

It should be apparent from this account of teleology that it cannot necessarily be equated with an inappropriate form of argument. It is generally accepted as an inevitable component of theism. Its role in certain theories of natural behaviour is more problematic but appears entrenched. For most students the interest in engaging teleology lies not in 'taking on' its established role in these areas but in identifying its power to mislead and misinform in fields where the tradition of explaining means by ends is weaker. In such contexts 'teleological' becomes a valuable term of criticism, one able to expose a failure to think clearly about causes and effects. The emphasis of such criticism should be on what an author gets wrong by being teleological.

Let's take an example from anthropology. Before proceeding it is necessary to point out that, within the social sciences, teleological analysis is often discussed as functionalism. There exists an ongoing debate within anthropology and sociology about the necessity or inevitability of explaining social processes and facts by reference to their function, their 'fit', within some wider system or structure. However, it is what such an approach does to the logical, theoretical and empirical content of one's argument, how teleology and functionalism can lead us astray and set up misleading tendencies within research, that is of interest to us here, rather than its inherent inadequacy.

To return to our example, imagine that you need to develop a critique of a model of familial relationships that claimed that their ultimate function – the goal of their design – was to ensure male dominance. Now this model may hold important clues to the topic; it may, indeed, be a significant advance in its field. However, it contains an inherently teleological/functionalist explanatory momentum (it might also strike you as simplistic, reductionist and determinist). It is true that one could dredge one's way through anthropological data from throughout the world, explaining all familial relationship types in terms of their 'fit' within this model and their functionality to the goals it establishes. But what would this prove? In criticising such an approach the terms teleological or functionalist may be usefully employed to highlight the way male dominance is posited as a kind of transcendental given, something that governs and defines everything else but is not itself subject to any such force. This general starting point should lead to more specific criticisms. For example, one might point out that certain family connections strengthen female rather than male power. One might also want to draw attention to all the other social relationships (for example those of class and ethnicity) that shape and structure the family. Either criticism would suggest that a teleological theory of male dominance leads to a distorted and limited analysis.

Care needs to be taken when using the term 'functionalism'. It is often used as a term of critique but it is also used as a descriptive label for forms of theory that explain events and processes by reference to structures. To avoid confusion you should be clear about your definition of the term.

• *Ad hominem*

Ad hominem is a Latin phrase meaning 'to the man'. Its most common usage is as a term of criticism for the notion that one can refute an argument by reference to the personal qualities of the person who espouses it. To see what is wrong with this idea imagine the following. You meet a trickster and famous liar who wishes to argue that $2 + 2 = 4$. Could you refute his mathematics by referring to his infamous conduct? Of course not. The latter would have no bearing on the logic and veracity of his position. Any such attempt would be *ad hominem*.

Partly because of its impersonal, formal nature, academic commentary is mercifully relatively free from crude examples of *ad hominem* arguments. However, within other areas, it abounds. Indeed, it is a staple of media and political debate.

The *ad hominem* approach can take a number of guises. The most crass examples are fairly easy to identify and dispute. However, it can have subtler forms, instances that are not so easy to condemn. Two of the most important are:

- **Arguments that test an individual's commitment** to a position by identifying possibilities within it that they may not have thought of and may find unacceptable (cf. *reductio ad absurdum* and **Socratic method**; see Glossary).

- **Arguments that are concerned with identifying contradictions** within someone's stated position or between their stated position and their actions (in political language, the target here is hypocrisy).

As far as the second instance is concerned, it is apparent that if the trickster's original argument was not that $2 + 2 = 4$ but that fooling people is wrong, he would be vulnerable to the charge of hypocrisy. The former of my two potentially justifiable examples of *ad hominem* works by directly testing the adequacy of an argument. For instance, to pursue our new example, one might want to see whether the trickster really did think tricking people was *always* wrong (even if not doing so would cost a life). Any concession on his part would mean that he might need to modify his position. Both examples are potentially revealing and offer legitimate and useful expressions of the *ad hominem* argument. However, both are often abused. Semantic trickery, especially in oral argument, can often get people to concede positions that they would not agree with in more reasonable and unharassed situations. Such disreputable practices have had the effect of creating suspicion around all forms of *ad hominem* argument. This might suggest that *ad hominem* is best used solely as a term of criticism and that students should steer clear of potentially doomed attempts to salvage it as a constructive form of argument. However, there is enough potential within the two forms mentioned above to suggest that this would be an overreaction. *Ad hominem* can, I would conclude, be both a term of criticism and a legitimate form of argument.

● Conclusion

I want to end this chapter where I began, with some words of caution. All the terms introduced in this chapter can be cast as 'weapons' of criticism. This is certainly how they are usually portrayed in law courts, in the media and in political debate. However, such military metaphors have their own destructive logic. After all, once one has blown the enemy away, what then? What have you got to look forward to – the day when you can dance on the bones of your defeated opponents; the day when everything is in ruins except your ego? The language of military conquest reveals an agenda in which victory is seen as an end in itself. The best way to avoid this kind of inanity is to make sure that your criticisms are part and parcel of a wider argument, that they feed into and inform your aims and ideals. It is the latter that should guide you, not the desire to generate criticism for its own sake.

Another word of caution may be mentioned here, one that touches on much wider issues concerning the way academics respond to criticism of themselves and of others. Academics tend to have a rather rosy self-image. They like to think they are impartial. Yet it would be absurd to pretend that their judgements are always determined by logic and clarity. All too often social prejudice can and does intervene. Discriminatory attitudes based on assumptions about political orientation, religious affiliation, gender, ethnicity and class can affect the way that arguments are received. These attitudes might not express themselves as crude hostility, indeed a patronising eagerness to concur and move rapidly on is often a more likely reaction. Yet, however it happens, the feeling that one is not being 'heard fairly' eats away at one's confidence. Although this book hasn't opened up this important topic, I would suggest that knowing the rules of effective argument provides a necessary resource for students wishing to resist being typecast or intimidated. The ideal of fair and constructive argument that exists within higher education actually offers the hope that such prejudices can be identified and expunged. I know universities and colleges can be flawed places. I know that academics aren't always the reasonable individuals that they would like us to believe. But, for all that, there remains a set of commitments concerning the form and nature of proper argument and the proper use of criticism that are still very much alive in higher education. More specifically, there exists a vision of argument as a learning experience and as something that should bring benefits not merely to the individuals involved but to the wider community.

 Practical tips

Basing an assignment largely or solely on criticism of somebody else's arguments is common practice. However, since it is a largely negative exercise it is more appropriate in shorter, more limited assignments (such as essays and exam responses) than in longer ones, such as dissertations.

Having to develop an argument about someone who is arguing about someone else, who is himself arguing about someone else who is ... can be bewildering! This intellectual equivalent of Pass the Parcel can easily produce a loss of confidence and focus. It is necessary to be ruthless at such moments and break the receding chain of argument as early as your central thesis allows. What this tends to mean in practice is either deleting all references to tangential or merely supplementary argument (i.e. writing as if it didn't exist) or restricting such references to short asides or footnotes.

 Exercises

1 Annotating an opinion piece

This is a short exercise (30 minutes) designed to get students talking and thinking about the act of criticism. All that is required is a short opinion piece on a broad, well-known topic from a recent newspaper or magazine. Individually or in twos or threes students need to read the piece and annotate it with criticisms. This is a quick exercise, so the emphasis is on writing as much as possible over and around the text. If the exercise is being done in a group then these annotations can be compared and the criticisms that have been produced ranked as more or less significant.

2 Listening and listing

The following exercise is an excellent way of starting to use and appreciate the intellectual tools discussed in this chapter. All it requires is an hour of your time, access to a television, radio or the internet, and a sheet of paper. On the latter you should write down, on the right-hand side and in column form, the key concepts discussed in this chapter (circularity, simplistic, reductionism and determinism, bias, teleology, *ad hominem*). Having done this you need to listen to and record 20 minutes of a discussion programme from the television or radio, or download a programme from the internet (if you use a DVD recorder remember this exercise is not about watching, it's about listening). It does not have to be a particularly serious or news-related programme but it does need to feature people talking (the fewer people the better: this exercise gets progressively more tricky the more voices you have to disentangle).

As you listen make a brief note, in the appropriate row, of the occurrence of any of the key concepts you have written down. These notes will need to be brief. For example 'X says apples are tasty because they have a great flavour', would go in the circularity row. You will find that some of your categories get filled up a lot more easily than others. Having completed your 20 minutes of listening and writing you should take 10 minutes simply to think about the discussion you have just heard. Ask yourself what was the general drift of the argument, what were the assumptions that were being made? These broader and underlying themes are often difficult to 'hear' the first time round. If, during this contemplative 10 minutes, you don't come up with anything, don't worry.

Now play your recording, or replay the programme online. This time around you should be doing two things:

- verifying that you placed your notes in the appropriate row;

- trying to find new examples of any of the key concepts on your list (especially those that you haven't found any illustrations of yet).

Believe it or not, this exercise can be quite fun. Played in pairs or in a group it can be made into a pleasant parlour game! A competitive element can be introduced by seeing who can find the greatest number of examples or, alternatively, who can find an example for the greatest number of categories. This exercise usually has the added pleasure of demonstrating that an awful lot of what people say on the television and radio makes very little sense.

3 Criticising your own work

What goes around comes around. If you are prepared to critique others then you should also be prepared to see your own work subjected to a similar level of scrutiny. This is one of those exercises that might seem an almighty hassle but can really pay off. Indeed it can make you see your work in an entirely new light. In this exercise all you will need is your last piece of written work and a red pen. The aim of the exercise is to see which forms of criticism your own work is *most* vulnerable to. I suggest you start off with the simpler criticisms to spot (over-simplification and reductionism), then move on to bias, *ad hominem*, determinism, teleology and circularity. Where you have identified a vulnerable passage, underline it in red.

If you are doing the exercise at all well, then you will end up with a lot of red on your work, particularly on those pages where you are explaining your argument. When this is done you can move on to the second part of the exercise: assessing how damaging these criticisms are. In note form on a separate sheet of paper, jot down answers to the following three questions:

- Does my (over-simplification, etc.) make my overall argument illogical?

- Does my (over-simplification, etc.) make my argument misleading or otherwise inaccurate?

- What realistic steps could I take to correct my (over-simplification, etc.)?

By the end of this exercise you should be in a much better position to assess in what area your work is particularly vulnerable to criticism and in what areas it is most robust and coherent.

5

Arguing out loud: oral presentations

How to stand up and deliver a convincing argument

Offering an argument to a live audience requires new skills. This chapter leads you through the necessary preparations as well as the structure that works best for oral presentations. We shall also review some of the concerns that people often have when facing the prospect of arguing out loud.

Key topics

- Preparing and structuring oral presentations
- Tips for the nervous
- Nasty questions
- Team presentations

Key terms
audiences emotions formats questions

Many of the worst presentations I have been to were delivered by people who were not in the least bit worried about speaking in public. They got up, smiled confidently and talked rubbish. Such folk will be aided by this chapter. But of course none of them will ever read it. They are, after all, insulated from doubt. And, in truth, I have a different reader in mind. A reader whose attitude more closely mirrors what is still the most common reaction to being required to talk in public – fear.

I will confess to another reason why I'm more sensitive to the problems of the timid than those of the fearless. For I, too, used to be mortified by the idea of opening my mouth in front of an audience. Moreover, I'd be lying if I claimed that I have since been reborn as an orator of repute. The prospect of speaking in front of a large group still makes me feel decidedly edgy. What matters though is that I can now handle such situations – they no longer frighten me in a way that is debilitating or paralysing. That's enough for me and it's enough for most students. For me this transition was the product of two things: practice, and feeling in control of my material. The frequency of readers' experience of oral presentations is not an issue I can do much about in this chapter. However, being in charge of your material is something I can help with.

Feeling that the situation is 'beyond you', that you are vulnerable and unaided, is the most important cause of anxiety in oral work. This emotion can be overcome and a sense of confidence gained by making sure that your argument is well prepared, well structured and sufficiently aided by visual materials. This chapter will explain how this can be done. Thus it will show you how to take control of your presentation and how to make sure your audience not only understands your argument but judges it to be clear and coherent.

● The preparation and structure of oral presentations

Student presentations are not required to make audiences roll to the floor with laughter or experience life-changing emotions. Self-dramatisation can be left to actors and media-literate politicians. What you are trying to do is something more mundane but, at the same time, more honest: to provide a reasoned argument that is both cogent and insightful.

The key difference between good oral and good written argument is that the former is **simpler**. This is true of content, of structure and of delivery. The reason **why** comes down to the difference between listening and reading. When we are reading something we can go at our own pace; we can return to points we find difficult to grasp first time around; we can take time to think. This whole process might take us hours, days, perhaps years. People do not sit in audiences for that long. Nor do they have instant recall. By the end of most presentations much of the audience will have forgotten what was said at the beginning. Indeed, some of them would have a hard time remembering the presenter's name or topic. Audiences cannot digest the level of complexity that is appropriate in written work. They need more repetition, more simplification, more help to understand.

Preparation for an oral presentation should not be rushed. Your confidence and your sense of control over your material will be considerably improved if you start preparing it at least a couple of days beforehand. Since simplicity and clarity are the key to good oral presentations, your preparations should be focused on removing confusion and ambiguity. The following model provides a guide to how to prepare effectively over a two-day period.

Day one

Work out your argument

Write it down in one sentence. With oral presentations you must make your argument as concise as possible. Ideally it should be articulated in only one or two clauses. Oral arguments favour short and bold statements. Whereas there is plenty of opportunity in written work for the use of numerous qualifiers and indications of provisionality, in verbal presentations such manoeuvrings can easily become confusing and tedious to audiences. A certain level of provocation, even to the point of slightly overstating one's case, is often exactly what is required to make people sit up and start listening to you.

Work out your structure

For a talk of about 15 minutes you will probably need three or perhaps four main sections. Shorter time periods may be divided into two. Anything over 20 minutes allows you to go up to five sections. However, this is the limit: any more than this and your talk will become list-like and confusing.

Reduce your material to notes

This is as necessary for PowerPoint users as it is for everyone else. From each of your sections take the key points and type them up. Key sentences that sum up whole sections or key ideas should be written down in full (these will need to be delivered with emphasis, so find a way of highlighting them). Do not be afraid of repeating key points. It is especially useful to repeat basic contentions made at the beginning sometime in the middle of your talk and then again at the end.

The start of your talk needs to include the same elements that commence any good essay. A statement of your central argument and a statement of the structure of your talk are both essential. Similarly, at the end you will need to return to these elements and make a concluding claim (for example, 'What I have shown in this talk ...', 'This confirms my original argument ...').

To avoid confusion, you will need to be ruthless about how many examples and how many digressions you are going to allow into your talk. Showing you appreciate such complexity cannot be done in the same way in oral presentations as it is in written work. In the former, all but the most central facts and theories must either be excluded or made marginal. Such marginalia should not be featured in your visual material but may be mentioned in asides. Such phrases as 'We know that Gilroy has explained ...', or 'I appreciate that Rousseau has offered a different perspective ...' – phrases that would seem too casual in written work – are quite acceptable in oral presentations. A similar point must be made about your treatment of facts. Long lists, of any sort, must be avoided. There is no way you are going to be able to cram in as much factual material as you can in a written piece. So don't try. Cull your facts until you have only the most exemplary and the most illuminating.

Working without PowerPoint

Good oral presentations rely on clear writing. You must be able to read your notes at a glance. If your handwriting is at all unclear you should write in capitals or get your notes printed. Using coloured highlighter pens helps to draw your eye to key phrases and passages. You may find writing your material on file cards convenient, especially if your presentation is to be delivered without the aid of a lectern. However, you don't want a stack of paper, of any sort, to deal with. A couple of sheets of A4 are more sensible than 50 fiddly file cards (and what if you drop them!). Keep the number of bits of paper you have to deal with to a minimum. And always number them very clearly.

Working with PowerPoint

As well as being a way of presenting slides to your audience, PowerPoint can be used to display your notes to yourself. However, while this option works well for some people it can exacerbate the unfortunate condition known as PowerPointitis. It is an unfortunate malady that causes presenters to be reduced to mere mouthpieces of the blue screen. Try not to hide behind PowerPoint. It is life-draining and slightly bizarre to watch someone read through vast numbers of PowerPoint slides (audiences can read too!). PowerPoint should be used as an aid, nothing more.

> The key slide in any PowerPoint presentation is the argument slide. ✔
> This should come near the start of your presentation and be written
> as one sentence in a clear, large font. It is helpful to label it 'Argument'
> or 'Thesis' or something similar. You may also wish to come back to this
> slide at the end of your talk.

Work out your visual aids

Whether it is PowerPoint slides, transparencies flapped on to an over-head projector or, even, chalk on a board, visual aids usually make a bigger impact than verbal information. The audience will interpret whatever you put up on the screen as key to your argument. Distracting them with irrelevant images is a bad idea.

For most 15-minute talks (especially ones that are not based on the analysis of visual material) I would suggest you use three to eight text-based images as well as one or two pictorial ones. These text-based aids are not transcriptions of your talk. If any one has more than 30 words on it you run the risk of losing your audience and interrupting the flow of the presentation. Choose a large font size and a clear font type. Remember, you will be reading out most or all of your text-based visuals. Your audience will both see them and hear them spoken. They need to be able to withstand a lot of scrutiny. Text-based visual aids often include the following:

- the title of your talk
- the structure of your talk (i.e. the titles of the different sections)
- a statement of your argument
- a statement relevant to each of your sections
- a concluding statement (this may simply involve reusing the title, structure or statement of argument).

Read your talk out loud

As you do so, pretend to be employing your visual aids. Talk in a clear and measured fashion. Time it. Pause repeatedly, placing emphasis on key words and phrases. Remember that it takes time to use and refer to visual aids. If your talk is only slightly under or over the time allocated then you can simply annotate your existing notes (deleting or adding one or two comments). If you are considerably over, then you may need to delete or considerably shrink a whole section. These are both relatively easy tasks. If you are considerably under the allocated time, then you have a larger problem. You will need to rethink what you are doing with the talk and perhaps change your central argument to accommodate a greater degree of depth (using another example or including an alternative perspective, for example).

Day two

Practise your talk

Ideally this should be done with a friend who can act as an audience. At this stage you should be practising looking at your audience and using your visual material as a prompt. Don't forget to pause and place emphasis on particular key passages. Take the practice seriously. Don't skip through it. Having gone through the whole thing beforehand provides a much greater feeling of control, ownership and, hence, confidence. Two or three run-throughs will be enough.

Prepare for questions

If questions are going to be asked after your presentation then you should make some notes beforehand based on the most likely ones to come up. Standard procedure here is to prepare for both the most obvious questions you can think of as well as the most difficult. You are far more likely to be confronted with the former. These often include things such as: 'Why did you choose to do this particular project?' and 'Can you tell us more about [a certain aspect of the presentation]?' Thinking about what the most difficult question someone could ask you would be is also useful, largely because it makes you feel that you are prepared for anything. Often the toughest questions are the shortest, for example, 'Does this matter?' or 'Is there anything new in what you are saying?' It is important not to react to these questions as if they were aggressive (even if they are). They require clear, positive answers, which will be all the more cogent for having been considered in advance.

You are not expected to deliver word-perfect answers to questions. Questions need to be answered directly, keeping eye contact with your audience, and with an enthusiastic, open attitude. Leafing through your notes to try and locate that perfect answer you wrote down two days ago breaks up the presentation and makes you look like you are not on top of your material. Far better to put your notes aside. They are now finished with. Be engaged with and interested in what your audience has to say and you will find that answering questions is not at all scary.

● Presentation day

If you have followed the steps outlined above then, come the day of your presentation, you will have a clear set of notes, a clear set of visual aids and some ready-prepared answers to likely questions. More importantly you will have a sense of confidence. You will have done 90 per cent of the hard work and have every reason to feel in control of the situation, even to enjoy it. A few things to remind yourself of as you begin:

- **Talk at a relaxed pace,** placing emphasis on key phrases and words. Oral presentations need to be delivered at a slightly slower rate than normal conversation. Avoid jokes to friends and self-deprecating remarks – they distract from your argument and are seen by examiners as a sign of nerves.

- **Both your central argument and the structure of your talk should be stated very early.** It is often a good idea to have memorised one sentence that neatly encapsulates your main point. This can then be delivered, more than once, without any reference to notes.

- When delivering key aspects of your talk you need to **make a special effort to engage your audience:** look directly at them and sound as if you mean what you say. Your body language can also assist you. Using your hands to emphasise points, even walking about a bit, can help to keep the attention of your audience.

- **Text-based visual material may be read out** to the audience. However, longer passages should be abbreviated. Remember to emphasise words and phrases that are particularly significant. Do not stand in front of your visuals or with your back to the audience. Unless you have some means of seeing both your visuals aids and your audience at the same time, you will need to be switching eye contact between the former and the latter.

- There may be moments when you need to **enliven your presentation** because you sense the audience is not really listening. This is especially likely towards the end of your talk and if there are other presenters waiting to go on. At such moments you need to spark your audience's interest by communicating the urgency and significance of your original argument. This can be done by summarising it in pithy language and indicating that your talk has reached its conclusion. You might also try raising your voice, making a bold gesture of the hands or using less formal language.

- If you find yourself in serious danger of **going well over the allocated time** the easiest thing to do is carry on as planned, up to a few minutes before your time limit, and then skip to your final and concluding section. This will avoid your having radically to restructure your talk on the hoof. If you are well under the allocated time then relax, speak a little more slowly, and expand on those aspects of your talk about which you feel confident.

- At the end **thank your audience.**

- **Your talk isn't over until you have answered the last question** posed by your audience. Resist the temptation to provide absurdly brief or jokey answers. You can undo all your good work at this point by not taking questions seriously. Phrases such as 'That's an interesting question ...' or 'That's a good question ...' may be appropriate. They flatter your audience and give the impression that you are listening. Try to draw questions, even tangled, long ones, back to your own material. If you don't understand a question, say so. If you feel you have the gist, but not much else, you may wish to paraphrase the question in your own terms, saying something like 'The point I take from your question is ...' or 'What you are asking is ...'. It is often useful to repeat your central argument during questions.

● Still worried? Tips for the nervous

It's OK to be nervous. It doesn't mean that anything is going wrong. Indeed it's those folk who are over-confident who should be concerned. What you want is not the absence of nerves but control over them. This requires the removal of the worry that you will flounder and panic. The answer, of course, is to make sure that nothing can go wrong. If you follow the steps outlined above you will have virtually ensured this. However, there remains the thorny issue of using notes as prompts. Professors and lecturers always encourage it, yet the reality is that many students don't find it easy. If it was so easy you would never get professors reading out their entire talk at academic conferences. The fact that this is not at all uncommon implies that, when confronted with their peers, academics are often just as nervous as students when confronted by theirs.

For those daunted by the prospect of relying purely on notes there are four options. The three that I don't recommend, but have seen work, are:

- just to read your paper (you may lose marks this way);
- to memorise huge chunks of your paper while having it in front of you as a back-up (this can be done but it is exhausting);
- to use prompt notes but have them annotated to enable you to refer to an easily accessible, full written version of your talk (sounds good in theory but is complicated in practice).

The approach I do recommend involves using a mix of prompt notes and reading. More specifically, short 'tricky bits' of your talk can be written out and read aloud and the rest assigned to notes. If you get it right, and look at your audience frequently while reading, this combination is indistinguishable from using prompt notes alone.

Something else that nervous students can do is to increase the number of visual aids. Lots of fancy images have the effect of taking the focus away from the presenter. The trend towards ever more complex, computer-based presentations is a godsend for those of a self-effacing disposition. Worried presenters should also prepare an impressive hand-out. This will guarantee that your audience will, one way or another, get your message.

● Nasty questions

Don't panic! It won't happen. Student presentations are very unlikely to elicit aggressive questions. But it's an eventuality that is worth taking a moment to consider, for two reasons. First, to reassure oneself that one really is prepared for anything. Second, because the gladiatorial argument culture that I complained about in the introduction to this book cannot just be ignored. If you come up against it you will need to be able to cope with its belligerent poses.

Nasty questions come in two flavours, abuse and refutation. Abuse is often based on prejudice. Some people may try to 'get at you' because of your perceived political views, age, gender, sexuality and so on. This might be combined with the use of insulting vocabulary to describe your argument. The thing to realise about abuse is that once you openly, publicly, identify it as abuse you regain control of the situation. Thus ideally one should stay calm and say something along the lines of: 'Your characterisation of my presentation as upper-class waffle is not an argument, it is merely invective'. It is not appropriate or necessary to launch a counter-offensive. Certainly, if you have condemned abuse as a form of argument, you shouldn't then contradict yourself by indulging in it.

A restrained response is also the best answer when challenged on your facts. My advice here is simple. Where you think your challenger is right, say so. Where they are wrong, tell them why. Where you don't know if they are wrong or right (and this is often the case – it is difficult to make accurate snap judgements on matters of any complexity), say something like, 'You may be right and if you are I will have to reconsider my position on that point' or 'I'll have to check that'. This may sound weak but in fact it will serve you much better than stubborn and egocentric defiance. Indeed, if you are engaged in a debate you should expect to concede points. After all, why should you know everything? Of course it's much easier to concede minor points than ones that are central to your argument. If the latter should ever befall you, 'I'll have to go away and consider that' is probably a better choice than 'Thank you for just demolishing my entire argument'.

> ✔ People worry about nasty questions but hardly ever get them. Far more common are *dull* questions which, if you answer them in a dull way, can provide a rather low note on which to end your presentation. Questions about minor points of methodology are some of the worst. A good tip is to answer the question but then add some intellectual value. For example, going on to say that 'what is really fascinating' about your material is what it tells us about your central argument.

● Team presentations

Team presentations require particular attention to structure and preparation. The different sections of the talk need to be allocated to team members. One person needs to be given the task of starting the presentation. They will provide the central argument as well as explain the structure of the talk. Someone also needs to have the role of timekeeper. This person, who will need to be in clear view of the speaker, should keep a track of the time during each section and indicate, in as non-obtrusive a fashion as possible, if anyone is over-running. Sections should be of roughly equal length. It is important that each of the presenters indicates their familiarity with the main argument.

The danger of teamwork is that only one or two people do the real work – i.e. developing the argument – and that the others just get drawn along, understanding very little about the aim of the project. Come presentation day this lack of cohesion may be revealed. The non-familiarised will sound precisely that. They will certainly have trouble with any questions that come their way. Thus it is necessary to make sure that each member of the team has learnt the central argument and that they all know, at the very least, how it relates to their specific section.

Team presentations require more time to prepare than individual talks. At least four meetings of the whole team are necessary. They also require a greater degree of concentration and 'professionalism' during the event. Team members need to look at the audience, not at each other, and resist the temptation to make asides among themselves.

● Finally … take it seriously

If you're reading this then you probably don't need to be told to take presentations seriously. But since, in my experience, it is the single biggest factor that undermines first-year student talks, I cannot finish this chapter without mentioning it. When confronted with an audience of your peers it is always going to be tempting to puncture the pomposity of the situation by playing it for laughs or to pile one's talk with self-deprecating asides. Maybe pomposity *should* be lanced in this way. Maybe people will enjoy your talk all the more for it.

However, these points count for little when set against the fact that what one communicates by this kind of conduct is that the topic under consideration is not really that important or interesting. If the presenter really doesn't care and isn't interested, then perhaps it is better that they subvert themselves and their talk than dissemble. But such people are clearly in the wrong place, certainly the wrong institution. Very few students are in such a position: most of us want to engage, to communicate seriously, because we do care, we are interested. The fact that presentations are often pompous occasions is, after all, a minor detail when compared to the significance of the material you are discussing. It is Third World debt, the rise of Romanticism, the effects of acid rain – *your* topics in all their diversity – that really matter. Everything else is piffle.

● Conclusion

There are many ways of presenting an effective talk. The model outlined in this chapter is designed to provide a useful pathway for inexperienced or unsure students. It shouldn't be interpreted as a set of fixed rules. Indeed, if all your peers start offering the same structure, the same format for their talks, then you are not going to win anyone's attention by doing exactly the same. More generally, your individuality, your personality, is always important in oral work; it is what makes your talk unique and it needs to be expressed if you are to avoid sounding like an academic clone. The latter fate is particularly frightening because academics are not the world's most accomplished presenters. Their gifts tend to lie elsewhere, in quiet study or analysis. Perhaps, as a consequence, few of them are so shallow as to think that presentation is as important as content. This fact should impress two things on you:

- Presentations must have a clear and well-developed intellectual agenda, they must have an argument;
- It really isn't that hard to do a decent presentation at college. You're not expected to bring the house down. You are expected to be intellectually engaged, clear and honest.

Practical tips

Presentations are performances. You should take them seriously but it is also important that you maintain as much eye contact with your audience as possible. Smiling, using your hands expressively, even occasionally walking up to your audience, can also help.

Some seasoned presenters develop verbal techniques to buy themselves time or allow them to reinforce a point. Pausing and then saying 'What am I saying? What I am saying is ...', is one example. 'So let's try and define that last point' is another.

Good presentations communicate enthusiasm. Useful phrases are 'What is fascinating about this ...', 'What I find really interesting about this ...', 'Why this is important ...'.

Exercises

1 A quick practice

This exercise is designed to provide a quick and painless practice for oral presentations. All it requires is a journal article, a notepad and one other person or an audio recorder. There are three parts to this exercise:

1. Fillet down your chosen journal article to note form. A really quick way of doing this is to highlight key passages and words. If the article does not have a stated central argument and structure you will need to provide these. This whole process need not take you more than 20–30 minutes.

2. Deliver a 10-minute talk based on your chosen article to your 'audience' (record it if necessary).

3. If you have a real-life audience they should be equipped with a notepad and be able to ask you one or two questions at the end and, perhaps, give you a mark. If you are using a recorder then don't listen to your talk straight away. Wait for a week and then listen to it (this gap will give you a bit of distance and objectivity), noting down any problems.

2 Performing on video

Recording yourself giving a presentation is one of the best ways of improving your technique. A commonly used exercise in tutorials is for students to video each other, then watch the recording as a group. However, you can also do this on your own or with a friend. Remember, you are not auditioning for your own chat show – presenters should look at their audience, not the camera, and should use visual aids, whether or not the camera manages to pick them up. What the recording is good at is showing the benefits of clear, unhurried and well-organised presentations. A checklist can help organise comments (whether from your peers or from yourself) on the strengths and weaknesses of your presentation (it does not address issues of content). Your checklist should include the following (where 1 is poor and 5 is excellent):

Clarity of argument	1	2	3	4	5	Comment:
Overall clarity	1	2	3	4	5	Comment:
Enthusiasm and conviction	1	2	3	4	5	Comment:
Use of aids	1	2	3	4	5	Comment:
Attention to audience	1	2	3	4	5	Comment:
Body language	1	2	3	4	5	Comment:
Response to questions	1	2	3	4	5	Comment:

6 | How to be original

Making your argument stand out

There are a number of straightforward ways that you can add originality to your argument. This chapter introduces a variety of techniques each of which has the potential to lift your assignment to a new level. The two simplest forms are addressed first ('new topics, comparisons and contexts' and 'minor to major').

Key topics
- New topics, new comparisons and new contexts
- Minor to major
- Theoretical collisions
- Listening for what is not being said
- Turning things on their head
- Doubt everything

Key terms
originality tradition fresh thinking

An argument that is new attracts attention. It can also attract higher marks. However, despite the value placed upon it, originality is rarely discussed as something that can be obtained or practised. Indeed, the opposite is often the case: although regarded as something that all students should aspire to, originality is presented as an innate capacity of the very few. Thus originality is dangled before the generality of students as a kind of talisman of the power and authority of their betters, the 'real thinkers', the 'real scholars' who form a tiny elite at the top of the discipline. As you might have guessed, I have little sympathy for such exclusionary rituals. I believe that originality is something that all students can have and develop. This conviction hasn't arisen from egalitarian wishful thinking. It has emerged from observing the way that, by doing very simple things and following very simple steps, even the most average of students can piece together not merely a coherent argument but also an innovative one.

This chapter will provide you with six ideas, six provocations, that can be employed to produce original analysis. They are designed to enable new angles, fresh lines of enquiry, to emerge in your work. The type of originality that can be assisted by these interventions is of a limited kind. Originality, as it is discussed here, is about taking an existing, recognised argument or approach, and mutating it. This mutation may involve inserting something into it, expanding some part of it, or twisting some aspect of it. What you are left with at the end is something both traditional and novel, a hybrid.

This may seem a rather unheroic notion of originality. However, it is at precisely this scale of innovation that most of the fêted scholars within your discipline will have worked. Don't confuse originality with having to rethink your entire discipline. It is something much more 'local' and much more achievable than that.

I'm not making a case here for modesty but for honesty. It is almost invariably more **accurate** to say something like 'This essay offers a distinctive contribution to the work that Patel and others have been pursuing', rather than 'This essay offers an argument without precedent or parallel'. The former formulation also helps one avoid accusations of **plagiarism** (see Glossary).

● New topics, new comparisons and new contexts

The easiest way to be original is by using new data to shed light on established theories. Many leading academics have made their reputations entirely through 'opening up' a new area in this way. This process can be broken down into new topics, new comparisons and new contexts.

New topics

New topics often come into view by chance. However, they are especially likely to be stumbled across by reading round one's area of enquiry or by drawing on one's personal interests. Both pathways tend to be obscured if you bury yourself too deeply and narrowly in an existing field. In other words, arriving at a new topic is often made easier if one steps back from the task at hand and asks some basic questions. These may include: 'What else could this theory explain?', 'What hasn't been investigated in this area?' and 'If I could write about what really interests me, what would that be?'

Such questions will elicit a variety of answers, many of little use. It is necessary to remember that new topics need to be of a substantive nature in order to be worth developing into arguments. Ideally they should be of a new type and concern an area of activity that has not been considered much, if at all, before. As this implies, taking a new example, however substantive, of an **established type** is a distinctly lesser form of originality.

This distinction can be better understood through an example. Imagine you are assigned a project on poverty in Africa. Trying to take a new angle, you may decide to focus your study on a country that has attracted relatively little attention in the English language literature, say Madagascar. However, comparable studies on other African countries are far from uncommon. Hence, although your project may achieve a certain level of interest because of the unusual nature of its example, it is not going to stand out as particularly original. In order to achieve that you will need to be much more innovative and find a topic that is not merely under-represented but that poses a new set of questions, a new framework within which to understand poverty in Africa. How about a project on African perceptions of the geography of poverty that would draw on the literature on mental mapping? Or a study of the notion of an Islamic tradition of understanding and explaining poverty in Africa? As these two examples suggest, new topics are often interdisciplinary in nature. They demand that you look beyond the traditions of your sub-field and draw in whatever material is necessary, from whatever source, to provide new insights into familiar questions. They also tend to be accompanied by a moment of panic. 'It sounds a great idea, but where would I find any information on that?' is a question that becomes a stumbling block for many a would-be original thinker. It is true that, occasionally, new topics do require new methodologies, new ways of defining what the relevant data are. However, a prosaic solution is usually at hand. If you are in the geography department and your new topic is taking you towards religious studies and history, then start digging in those literatures. If you're in English studies and the novelty of your topic relies on its anthropological content, then it's time you visited a different section of the library. Originality does not dispense with existing traditions, but connects them.

New comparisons and new contexts

All scholarship requires comparison and context. However, there are familiar and orthodox forms of both within most fields. These traditions are seen within the thing to be compared or contextualised and the unit or scale of comparison or contextualisation. For example, within English literature the thing to be compared is often the novel, the scale is frequently the nation and the context is usually the modern period. Thus essays on the rise of the novel in nineteenth-century Britain and France are staple fare. Originality in argument can be achieved by changing and, at least by inference, challenging, any or all of these factors. A common way of doing this is to take a subject usually addressed within the context of one historical period or one geographical area and look at it in a very different period or area. For example, if the rise of the novel is usually considered in the context of Western societies then exploring this subject outside the West might be original. Similarly, if non-mythological fictional, plot-based narratives are usually addressed within the context of modern history, it may be original to see if prototypical forms existed in medieval or ancient societies.

However, one needs to be careful when developing new comparisons and contexts that they provide you with something interesting to say. Comparing the rise of the novel in India and Thailand may not have been done before. But, unless this comparison contributes to the wider debate, unless these national histories offer fresh insights, whether on a regional or global scale, then such an attempt at originality is likely to appear arbitrary, even tokenistic. Perhaps a more substantive intervention into this particular debate would not be to choose countries that 'haven't been done', but to alter the unit or scale of analysis. For example, one might want to consider how the existing critical literature in the area is premised on ideologies of 'Westernness' and 'non-Westernness'. Scale is most easily understood in its geographical sense (for example locality, region, nation, continent). However, geography is just one way of drawing up boundaries around what interests us. The broader concept of 'unit of analysis' brings into view a much wider set of possibilities. Another instance from English literature will help to explain the point. The traditional units of analysis discussed in this field are the individual (especially the author), the group or movement of authors, the readership and the nation. Other units of analysis familiar today include gender (for example, women's literature), class and race. However, there are plenty of other ways of drawing up one's parameters of enquiry, such as perhaps the family (as reader or author) and the publishing industry, which might also provide interesting material for context and comparison.

● Minor to major

The most interesting things within a book are often those that get the slightest treatment. Footnotes, minor examples and tangential remarks can all be memorable precisely because they are concisely phrased and stick out from the main flow of the text. Such material is at its best when it makes you want to pursue it further, to transform it from a detail to something deeper and more complex. This desire may lead nowhere. It may result in you ferreting around for months after information that was only ever worth a glancing reference. And yet it is not a desire that should ever be discouraged. For following up such minor themes can provide insights into one's field that are not merely fresh but which usefully question and throw into relief the set of priorities that are at work within it. Moreover, it is pertinent to observe that the themes that dominate debate today are usually ones that had a marginal existence in the research of the past. It seems reasonable to suppose that the dominant foci of future study, if they are being anticipated at all, exist within the marginalia, the footnotes and subtexts of today's literature.

The question thus becomes, 'Which details, which minor themes, are worth exploring further?' As I've already implied, if you get this question right, your work is likely to be seen as making a substantial and original contribution. If you get it wrong, your contribution will, at best, be seen as eccentric ('original' but not in the sense you would have hoped for). What you should be looking for are ideas that contain potential, that have the makings of something more significant. The easiest way of spotting such themes is to look for those facts and ideas that are flagged by authors as potentially substantive but noted as being beyond the remit or capabilities of their study. By contrast, the clearest examples of themes that should be left well alone are those that have the quality of throw-away remarks, digressions that arise from mere whim. Similarly unpromising are those asides or footnotes that amount to potted literature summaries, designed essentially to demonstrate the comprehensiveness of the author's reading. Minor themes that are worth pursuing tend not to be circumscribed in this way. They provide open doors, not fixed solutions, clues to the existence of other pathways through the material.

✔ Make it clear that what you are doing is original. Phrases that may be useful include: 'This theme has been marginalised in the previous literature'; 'References to this theme are scarce and scattered'.

● Theoretical collisions

Originality is usually based on a knowledge of tradition. Without appreciating what has gone before it is difficult to know how to be innovative. In this regard ignorance can, unfortunately, be bliss: there are many people who regard their ideas as terrifically bold and new precisely because they have never bothered to investigate their antecedents. Understanding what has gone before is especially important when one is claiming theoretical originality. Because of its abstract nature theoretical work, however novel it seems, tends to have echoes or similarities with previous approaches that went under a different name. Far from undermining your work, showing that you appreciate these similarities and overlaps establishes its seriousness.

Theoretical innovations occur in many ways. However, one of the easiest and most productive is by collision. Mixing and splicing theoretical traditions together can enable a more sophisticated, as well as a new, way of explaining a particular topic. Many of the most celebrated theories of the last century arose from this process. Sartre's Marxist existentialism, Giddens' theory of structuration and Wallerstein's world systems theory all derived from creatively mixing existing approaches. These may seem rather grand examples but, at root, this isn't a process that is necessarily daunting or incredibly complex. One of the simplest ways of travelling this path is to structure one's studies around the claim that you have identified a theory which, while not new in itself, is new in one's discipline and has a contribution to make to it. For example, although geography is a theoretically very diverse subject, there has been little work within it originating from a psychoanalytical perspective. The question thus becomes 'What contribution could such a perspective make to the study of geography?' As it turns out, and as some recent writers in this discipline have come to accept, there are a range of insights that psychoanalysis provides on such issues as urban form and use, and cultural landscapes.

The pursuit of theories 'out there' that have a possible contribution to your discipline or sub-field should not be done for its own sake. More specifically, dragging in irrelevant and/or half-understood material merely because it appears novel is likely to lead to disaster. However, if you give proper consideration both to the identification of the existing theories in your area and to the nature of the 'theoretical import' you are contemplating, this approach provides an exciting and relatively simple way of saying something new and important.

● Listening for what is not being said

A familiar component of everyday arguments is the assertion that what someone is not saying is more important, more revealing, than what they are actually saying. This idea is just as common within academic debate. Listening for absences, for unspoken assumptions and marginalised facts, can provide powerful critiques and enable the identification of substantive new areas of enquiry. As this suggests, 'listening for what is not being said' has two aspects: criticism and the formation of new research agendas. Just how likely either emphasis is to lead to something original depends on your choice and treatment of the theme to be 'revealed' or 'uncovered'. For example, although pointing to the series of silences around the subject of gender and women in the work of the scholar of orientalism Edward Said may lead towards a substantive and interesting essay, it would not be original. Many people have noticed that particular absence before. Remember, 'listening for what is not being said' is a familiar academic technique. Indeed it is good practice to expect that one's attempts in this area will, in some way, be derivative, and so you need to qualify heavily any claims to innovation. Moreover, merely noticing that someone has not said or done something is not, in itself, of interest or importance. The familiar annotation of 'So what?' is all you can expect if you fail to accompany your observations with a clear rationale (why are you picking out this absence?) and analysis (what are you going to argue about this absence?).

These warnings should make it clear that being original by 'listening for what is not being said' requires a lot of thought and careful study. Nevertheless, some initial ideas on what aspects of a topic to pursue in this fashion can be jotted down very quickly (see Exercise 1). It is usually worth trying such possible routes, at least for a short while, just to see where they might go.

● Turning things on their head

Traditions do not survive because people identify them, discuss them and agree to their continuation. They survive, for the most part, because people don't do any of these things; they are sustained because they are treated as obvious, common sense and beyond discussion. Thus it is not always easy to think about the conventions of one's discipline. They tend to be invisible or only discussed in certain 'routinised' ways. This is the context that makes the practice of challenging the dominant order of knowledge so iconoclastic. 'Turning things on their head' is a specific but potentially extremely effective way of mounting such a challenge. The most well-known instances of this practice concern the issue of causality. For example, in the eighteenth and nineteenth centuries the idealist argument that certain abstract ideas shaped material reality was turned on its head by the empiricist and materialist assertion that the opposite was true, i.e. that the material realities of the world established the dominant ideas. However, turning things on their head doesn't have to involve such abstract concerns. Indeed, more particular instances are more common. Consider, for example, the explanation of poverty in the Third World. The traditional 'Western explanation', developed during the colonial era, was that poverty was caused by certain inadequacies within primitive cultures and that colonial contact was necessary in order to assist in the development process. However, this position was challenged by the assertion that it was Western colonialism that caused the poverty and which 'underdeveloped' the Third World. What this and other examples teach us is that the effectiveness and utility of 'turning things on their heads' depends on:

- being able to identify and challenge an existing and dominant assumption about causality;
- being able to explain why the reasoning behind this assumption is back to front.

● Doubt everything

Doubt has many faces. It can be a cowardly and indecisive position, a refusal of commitment. It can also appear as heroic, a daring challenge to established and dominant ideas. The role of doubt in academic debate simultaneously sustains both these tendencies. The ubiquitous notion that science and social science aspire to an 'organised scepticism', that academics are in the business of **questioning**, suggests a desire to be seen as standing up against the authority of traditional knowledge. Yet doubt in academic debate also works in the other direction: it undermines convictions, subverts the desire to prioritise one thing over another and encourages an attitude of aloof indifference.

This tension should be borne in mind when you hear professors issue the bold challenge to 'doubt everything'. It certainly suggests that this maxim should not be read naively. You are not being invited to rise up against anything. Nevertheless, what you are being encouraged to do remains extraordinarily exciting and intellectually liberating – to understand the ideas and terms that you are learning about, not as givens, but as constructs, things that can be questioned and challenged.

Such a task can never be completed. It is an attitude to knowledge, a way of thinking that **continuously** exposes and disturbs orthodoxies. This may sound bewildering and unsettling. However, it is important to recall that it is something that students do all the time. Questioning one's material is what being a student is all about. The challenge is to take this process further, to doubt not merely those things that have been flagged up for you as problematic but also those terms and concepts that appear to have escaped inspection and exploration.

Practical tips

With claims to originality, less is often more. The more limited and precise your claim is, the more convincing it will be.

Make sure you flag up clearly the nature and limits of your claim to originality. Just 'doing Madagascar' is not enough, you have to make it clear that this country has not been considered before and why it is important to do so now.

It is often appropriate to build on a new topic, theme or technique in your other assignments. Rather than search for something original for every new assignment you can develop (*not* just repeat) the new topic, theme or technique you developed earlier and in this way make it your own.

Exercises

1 Brainstorm

This is a short (30 minutes) brainstorming exercise. It is designed to blow away some of the hesitancy and reserve with which we often approach academic material. It needs to be pitched around a well-known topic within your area of study or expertise. Once this has been chosen, all that is required is that individually, or within a group, ideas about new ways this topic could be approached are thrown out in profusion and noted down. This is a 'say anything', inevitably irreverent, exercise and should not be judged a failure if the results are not particularly intellectually impressive. If you can circle just one idea that emerges that could be called, or might eventually become, substantive, then that's a bonus.

2 Thinking up new approaches

This exercise is designed to get you to think up some new lines of inquiry within a particular area of study. Although what emerges from it may not be substantive or usable, it should encourage a sense of confidence in your powers of imagination and creativity.

It is important to start with the right frame of mind before undertaking this exercise. You need to stop thinking about how your responses will be perceived and focus on simply writing down as much material as possible. The more angles and ideas you come up with, the more successful the exercise has been.

To start, you need to frame a simple question, preferably one that is open to many answers. A good example would be a question that asks for a definition of something complex, such as: 'What is unemployment?' Taking no more than 20 minutes, and using note form, write down as many different responses to your question as possible. Your answer can be as personal or as abstract as you like. Try to write down at least 30. Some of your responses will be daft and some won't.

Now scribble out all those responses that you judge to be familiar and recognised components of existing debates on the topic. You may finish the exercise at this stage, perhaps using the remaining answers as a basis for a group discussion. However, if you want to stretch yourself you can take things further. Of those responses left, circle two that strike you as promising or particularly interesting. With reference only to these two ideas, write a short paragraph explaining the occurrence and nature of the phenomenon that you are exploring. However usable the final product turns out to be, what you will have achieved if you complete this exercise is something quite remarkable. You will have put convention aside and worked out the beginnings of a different type of approach, a different set of priorities.

3 The value of doubt

> I who have no party to defend adopt the method of Absolute Doubt and apply it first of all to civilisation and to its most deeply rooted prejudices.
>
> (Charles Fourier, 1972; originally published 1808)

In this exercise you are required to scrutinise a piece of academic writing. The aim of the exercise is to subject your object of analysis to as much doubt as possible. By the end of it you should feel both more circumspect about the truth claims contained within it and more inclined to think there may be alternative ways of responding to the issues that it engages.

What you are going to be looking for are the assumptions upon which your chosen article is based. The piece of work in question should be short and self-contained. One of your own essays would be an acceptable choice. However, remember that the closer the piece is to you and your discipline the more difficult it is going to be to 'see the wood from the trees', i.e. to identify the conventions that structure and guide it. Once you have chosen your piece, but before reading through it, divide up a piece of paper with between two and all of the following headings:

- **Assumptions about categories:** The way data and ideas are labelled, boxed together as the same thing.

- **Assumptions about audience:** What is being taken for granted in respect of the level and type of expectation and education that readers bring to the piece as well as the nature of their response.

- **Assumptions about significance:** What is being accepted about the importance of the research and its findings.

- **Assumptions about authority:** The way other material is referenced in the piece, more especially the acceptance of certain ideas and findings that are not evidenced or proven in the piece itself.

- **Assumptions about causality:** The beliefs about why and how one thing follows another that are accepted and sustained by the piece under review.

These headings are designed to structure your examination of the assumptions found within the article with which you are working. They are not all-inclusive. Many assumptions will be missed. However, they will serve to structure your response and to remind you that assumptions take a variety of forms. I've suggested that you may want to choose fewer than five of these headings because this exercise is not easy, at least not if you do it well. If preceded by a discussion of the meaning of the categories listed, this exercise is easily adapted to group work.

AFTERWORD, REFERENCES, FURTHER READING AND GLOSSARY

Afterword

● Having something to say

Believing that one has something to say can be very hard. It's easy to drift through life convinced of one's inadequacy, convinced that in order to have something to say one has to be extraordinarily articulate, rich and aggressive. A corollary of this belief is the rather pitiful notion that, in order to be taken seriously, one has to emulate the style and methods of the 'people who matter'. One has to become self-serving, evasive, and prepared to get one's way at any price. In this context, learning how to argue can seem pretty much the same thing as learning how to be cruel. It is a depressing prospect and, ironically, produces people who, far from having something to say, have absolutely nothing to say except 'Look at me' and 'I'm better than you'.

This book is designed to show students how to argue, but it also has another ambition. For throughout it is woven an argument about arguing. My two basic assertions have been both descriptive and prescriptive. The first is that argument need not and should not be about domination and one-upmanship. The ideal of argument in academia offers an alternative model. For it presents argument as a learning process, a form of constructive engagement designed to lead towards insight and illumination. Admitting one is wrong and listening to others are integral components of this process. Far from being signs of weakness they indicate seriousness and rigour. Of course, this ideal is not confined to academics, and I suspect it is what most people would want and expect from good argument. However, higher education remains one of the few areas where it is openly celebrated and where it retains an institutional base. More than that, the distinctiveness of higher education, what it has to offer society, is rooted in this model of debate. As this suggests, it is important that students feel they have a stake in this ideal, that they regard it as something to value and use.

The second argument that has emerged in this book arises from the first. It is, simply, that argument can and must be taught and practised. Such a stance may sound commonsensical. However it is an unfortunate reality that argument is becoming marginalised in higher education. In many countries the focus is now on teaching basic 'key skills', such as numeracy, literacy, group work, timekeeping and computer skills. These are all necessary but none develops or sustains what is distinctive or vital about higher education. Indeed, since they could all be acquired elsewhere (for example, in secondary education or through other forms of training), to lay too much emphasis on them undermines the purpose and point of tertiary education. Currently an unsustainable tension exists between these competing visions of the university. On the one hand students are still required to produce arguments, indeed arguments remain by far the most important things to understand and learn in most courses. On the other hand argument is rarely taught or clearly acknowledged – all too often it is obfuscated by being presented as tremendously difficult or mysterious. I have sought in this book to show that learning how to argue isn't beyond anyone. It isn't something that requires one to stare into the misty distance in search of inspiration or spend one's youth growing pale and ill inside some enormous library. It may seem harder than the 'key skills' mentioned above (although this isn't saying much), but it is precisely because people want an intellectual challenge that they go to university.

None of the advice I've offered in this book will necessarily solve the dilemma I posed at the start of this afterword. When asked for one's view, one's particular perspective, it is easy to doubt that one has any such thing. As a consequence people retreat into embarrassed silence or, more depressingly, self-mockery and irony. This feeling of inadequacy is sustained by the widespread idea that intellectual activity springs from an entirely internal source. Panning one's private thoughts for gold, digging deep into one's psyche for nuggets of original opinion, are lonely pastimes. And for most of us the end product is nothing more than a feeling of emptiness. The truth is you don't have it in you. But then that's hardly surprising, because *you* are the wrong place to look. Arguments don't come from within. They arise from an engagement with issues and facts, from the way people live their lives and go to their deaths, from what goes on beyond the confines of your skull. To argue is to be in the world, to be involved. Seen in this way it becomes a lot easier to realise that the fact that you care about certain issues, the fact that you believe that certain ideas are important or need exploring, *is* to have something to say. More than that, it is to understand that your arguments are worth expressing, that they actually, seriously, honestly, matter.

References

Bacon, F. (1985) *The Essays*. London, Penguin.

Bartlett, R. (1993) *The Making of Europe: Conquest, Colonization and Cultural Change 950–1350*. London, Penguin.

Fourier, C. (1972) *The Utopian Vision of Charles Fourier: Selected Texts on Work, Love and Passionate Attraction*. Boston, Beacon Press.

Huxley, J. and Haddon, A. C. (1935) *We Europeans: A Survey of 'Racial' Problems*. Harmondsworth, Penguin.

Mander, A. (1936) *Clearer Thinking*. London, Watts & Company.

Maury, M. (1874) *The Physical Geography of the Sea*. London, Nelson.

Spence, G. (1995) *How to Argue and Win Every Time: At Home, At Work, In Court, Everywhere, Every Day*. London, Macmillan.

Wilde, O. (1912) *The Importance of Being Earnest*. London, Methuen.

Further reading

Books about argument seem to fall into one of two main types: mass-market and lightweight or academic and incredibly heavy. Some of the more useful and accessible titles from both categories, as well as a few that have managed to escape either fate, are listed below.

Billig, M. (1996) *Arguing and Thinking: A Rhetorical Approach to Social Psychology: New Edition*. Cambridge, Cambridge University Press.

Cottrell, S. (2005) *Critical Thinking Skills: Developing Effective Analysis and Argument*. London, Palgrave.

Davies, J. and Bickenbach, J. (1996) *Good Reasons for Better Arguments*. Peterborough, Broadview Press.

Dewy, J. (1933) *How We Think: A Restatement of the Relation of Reflective Thinking to the Educative Process*. Boston, D. C. Heath.

Fairbairn, G. and Winch, C. (1996) *Reading, Writing and Reasoning: A Guide for Students*. Philadelphia, Open University Press.

Hart, C. (1998) *Doing a Literature Review: Releasing the Social Science Research Imagination*. London, Sage.

McInerny, D. (2005) *Being Logical: A Guide to Good Thinking*. New York, Random House.

Siegel, H. (1988) *Educating Reason*. New York, Routledge.

Tannen, D. (1998) *The Argument Culture: Moving from Debate to Dialogue*. New York, Random House.

Thomson, A. (1996) *Critical Reasoning: A Practical Introduction*. London, Routledge.

Thouless, R. and Thouless, C. (1990) *Straight and Crooked Thinking*. Sevenoaks, Hodder & Stoughton.

Toulmin, S. (1958) *The Uses of Argument*. Cambridge, Cambridge University Press.

Glossary

An adequate argument requires an adequate vocabulary. This glossary provides definitions of the key terms with which anyone engaged in academic argument should be familiar. I've also included some phrases that are rarely used but which I judge to be revealing and potentially useful. These terms, which should never be used without a clear explanation of what they mean, are marked 'rare'.

ad hominem (Latin: to the man) A term of criticism for the notion that one can refute an argument by reference to the personal qualities of the person who espouses it. See Chapter 4 for discussion.

Anachronism The product of attributing something to an historical period where it does not belong. Within academic work, the problem of anachronism pertains, largely, to conceptual matters. For example, if we accept that 'racism' (defined as the assertion of natural differences and inequalities between objectively different human types) is a modern invention, then we must conclude that any study of ancient or medieval societies that employs the concept is guilty of anachronism.

Analogy A claim of similarity between two apparently dissimilar things. Analogies are common devices within argument. More specifically, the observation that something is like something else is used in arguments that proceed by analogy, as the basis for claiming that these two somethings must be similar in other respects. Analogies are often unreliable. They can be claimed to be suggestive and interesting but arguments that are rooted in them are likely to be misleading.

Analysis A detailed examination of the constituent elements of something. As this implies, an analysis can be purely descriptive. However, within the social sciences and humanities, the term is often used as a synonym for argument. Thus, in these fields, analysis has come to be equated with an explanation of how and why something is the way it is.

Anthropomorphism The act of attributing human properties to non-human things. The error of anthropomorphism usually occurs when research applies human emotions and experiences to the non-human (for example, imagining that animals fall in love or that nation states have 'life cycles').

Argumentum ad baculum (rare; Latin: argument appealing to the stick) An argument that uses threat. In academic life it is not usually a literal stick that is wielded. However, political, moral and economic threats are not uncommon. For example, 'All those who oppose me have no place in this institution', or 'Only Fascists will find any objection to my argument'.

argumentum ad populum (rare; Latin: argument appealing to the people) A form of argument designed to appeal to the crowd. The term is also used for the notion that if an idea is widely believed it should be considered true.

argumentum ad verecundiam (rare; Latin: argument appealing to respect) An argument based on an appeal to authority. Academic arguments often rely on appeals to the authority of secondary sources. An *argumentum ad verecundiam* is an exaggerated form of this tendency. Such arguments are characterised by the unsubstantiated, cavalier assertion that something is so simply because a named authority says so.

Bias To have a bias is to have a specific disposition, or prejudice, in favour of certain interpretations of events and against others. As a general rule, the term should be avoided in favour of more specific criticisms. See Chapter 4 for discussion.

Case study Provides a detailed study of an instance of a wider phenomenon. Case studies are not necessarily representative or typical. However, by offering an in-depth understanding of the complexities of a single event, they can provide insights and a richness of detail unavailable to broader surveys.

Circularity A term of criticism for arguments where the first claim is proved by reference to a second claim that depends on the acceptance of the first claim. For example, 'The existence of a personal God is proved by the Bible; and the authority of the Bible must, of course, be accepted because it was inspired by God'. See Chapter 4 for discussion.

Circumlocution As the term implies, circumlocution refers to the practice of speaking around a topic rather than about it. The word is used to describe verbosity and/or the act of avoiding and evading a subject by not addressing it directly and clearly.

Comparison Comparative arguments analyse a phenomenon in the context of a separate but in some way similar phenomenon. One of the most popular forms of comparative argument is geographical, the comparison of one place with another. See Chapter 1 for discussion.

Conflate A term of criticism identifying the practice of treating two or more separate things as if they were one.

Contradiction The mutual opposition of two things (for example events, processes, ideas). See Chapter 1 for discussion.

Counterfactuals Alternative, historical scenarios based on extrapolating real facts and inventing others. Counterfactuals are constructed from creative responses to the question 'What if ...?'. Counterfactuals are cumbersome devices and inherently unreliable.

Critical The term has two meanings: a) a form of evaluation that seeks to identify, uncover and, sometimes, counter assertions and assumptions; b) negative judgement. The term sometimes carries political connotations since it has often been used to challenge orthodox assumptions.

Criticism In the humanities, criticism is often used to refer to the process of analysis and debate (for example, literary criticism). In the social sciences criticism is usually used in its more popular sense, as referring to a negative judgement.

Critique An argument, usually taking the form of a critical (see **critical**, meaning a) exposition.

Deconstruction A technique of analysis that emphasises the inadequacy, fluidity and interdependency of categories and meanings. See Chapter 1 for discussion.

Deduction The process of arriving at a generalised conclusion by formulating a thesis or hypothesis then testing it against empirical data (cf. **induction**). The term may also be used to describe the act of inferring particular instances from a general law. See Chapter 1 for discussion.

Definition A verbal encapsulation of the exact meaning of a term or idea. Because so many words have multiple and diverse meanings, in argument it is usually helpful to define one's key categories.

Determinism The conviction that events are predetermined. Extreme determinists believe that everything that does happen was bound to happen. This notion removes the possibility of human choice and contains the implausible implication that the future is, or could be, entirely predictable.

Devil's advocate To play devil's advocate is to take a contrary position either for its own sake or, more usefully, for the purpose of identifying and exploring problems within another's argument.

Dialectic Now generally employed to describe a contradictory process. A dialectic involves three things: a) something (a thesis); b) its opposite (an anti-thesis); c) the synthesis of this contradiction. Thus to call something dialectical is to identify a movement from thesis and anti-thesis to synthesis. See Chapter 1 for discussion.

Dogma A principle or set of principles established by and reliant on the authority of religion. The term is also used to refer to any set of ideas that are adhered to in a stubborn and blinkered fashion. Dogmatism is antithetical to argument.

Elenchus (rare) A form of refutation (associated with Socrates) of an interlocutor's argument by means of gaining their assent to a further proposition that is inconsistent with their position.

Epiplexis (rare) A form of argument that tries to shame or chide people into agreement. It is often expressed through morally loaded rhetorical questions.

Epistemology A theory of knowledge. Epistemological questions are those that concern how and why something is known.

Eristic (rare) A form of argument designed to achieve, not truth or coherence, but victory in debate.

Ethnocentrism Bias in favour of a particular ethnic group. The most common forms of ethnocentrism are often the least noticed.

Evidence Arguments based upon empirical claims require evidence. It is expected that when seeking to establish an argument the arguer will have looked at as much relevant evidence as possible, both supportive and non-supportive. However, even when this has been done, it is usually good practice to imply a level of provisionality to one's conclusions. Thus one's argument should not close off the possibility of new evidence or evidence that has escaped one's attention. Within most fields of enquiry evidence takes the form of material that is suggestive of a particular conclusion rather than simply proves it. See Chapter 2 for discussion.

Fact A fact is always a claim. The claim may concern a verifiable, objective truth and/or an experience. Throughout academia, the notion that facts 'speak for themselves' is associated with naive, inductive arguments.

Faith A truth claim that is narrated as a deep belief and, hence, claimed to be beyond the normal rules of evidence and/or rationality.

Functionalism A functionalist is someone who explains a process or event by reference to its function within some overarching and determining structure or end point (functionalism, in this sense, is a form of teleology).

Hyperbole An exaggerated statement. The term is useful in criticising arguments that overstate their case or exaggerate the significance of their evidence.

Hypothesis A speculative proposition (cf. **thesis**). An hypothesis is not a truth claim but rather a testable starting point for an investigation or debate. Hypotheses can be proven or falsified. However, it is often more useful to adapt them, using one's evidence to alter one's original hypothesis in order to create another, more promising one. Although useful in many areas of study, it is important to appreciate that the practice of 'testing hypotheses against evidence' is a scientific methodology that is widely considered to presume that what one is studying takes the form of objective and quantifiable facts. The more interpretative one's material, the more it concerns social meaning, the less appropriate it is to formulate the starting point of one's work as a hypothesis.

Hypothetical This term has two principal meanings: a) describing an hypothesis or the reasoning that led to an hypothesis; b) an imagined example or event extrapolated from known facts (see also **counterfactuals**).

Ideal speech situation A term, derived from the work of the philosopher Jürgen Habermas, for an interchange of ideas in which all parties are fully informed, acting as equals and striving towards the truth.

idée fixe (French: fixed idea) Where an argument centres on a dominating and unshakeable conviction, this may be termed its *idée fixe*. Although the term can be used descriptively and without critical intent, it can also be used to imply an obsessive, monomaniacal narrowness of vision.

Ideology Although sometimes used to describe any interconnected set, or pattern, of opinion, 'ideology' and 'ideological' are best known today as terms of political criticism, applied to views that are considered by their opponents to be doctrinaire and misguided.

Idiographic The description of the unique (cf. **nomothetic**). Idiographic approaches imply the validity of detailing unique instances and the difficulty or impossibility of arriving at universally valid laws.

Induction The process of arriving at a generalised conclusion on the basis of observation (cf. **deduction**). See Chapter 1 for discussion.

Invective Abusive and attacking words. To accuse someone of using an invective is to claim that their argument is both unreasonable and objectionable.

Logic The process of reasoning. More specifically, logic concerns the way one thing is understood to follow, or connect to, another. All arguments contain a claim to logic. One of the principal tasks of the critic is to determine the veracity and appropriateness of such claims. This task is complicated by the existence of different types and expectations of logic. At one extreme, in some forms of study, logic is equated with the production of incontrovertible statements (for example, see **syllogism**). By contrast, in other (far more common) areas of endeavour, logic is understood to be present whenever 'persuasive' or 'reasonable' conclusions are drawn by way of implication and generalisation.

Metaphor A figure of speech in which something is described in terms of something else. For example, 'her labyrinthine mind' or 'his argument crumbled'.

Methodology An account of method. Methodology refers to the question 'How?' (cf. **theory**). Thus, for example, the way you carry out a piece of writing or research is your methodology. However, any *selection* of methodology is always a matter of both theory and practice. Moreover, methodologies are based on an interpretation of the nature and status of one's evidence. Thus, one's choice of research methodology needs to be justified and explained in the context of both one's data and theoretical approach.

Metonymy A figure of speech in which the name of a characteristic of a thing is substituted for the thing itself, for example calling the royal family 'the Crown'.

Nomothetic The study of universal laws (cf. **idiographic**). Nomothetic approaches assert the primacy of finding universal laws over the detailing of unique instances.

non sequitur (Latin: it does not follow) Used to describe a sudden and, perhaps, illogical transition from one idea to another, completely different, one.

'no true Scot' move (rare) A philosophical nickname for arguments based on a fiction of authentic identity. This type of argument relies on a claim to have identified the essence of a phenomenon. However, it is the evasiveness of this putative essence that makes the 'no true Scot' move a term of criticism. The term derives from a hypothetical exchange in which one party claims that no Scot would do x. Their interlocutor notes 'But one did.'. The first party tries to counter by claiming 'that no *true* Scot' would do x. The 'no true Scot' move represents evasion disguised as insight.

Objective This term is usually equated with actually existing reality: the real facts that are external to human interpretations and emotions (cf. **subjective**).

Ontology A theory of the nature of being. Ontological questions are those that concern the explanation of something's existence and primordial characteristics.

Oxymoron A figure of speech that is a contradiction in terms; for example 'a brave coward'.

Panegyric A fulsome statement of praise. The term often carries a critical edge, implying that a more balanced statement is more appropriate.

Paradigm This term is used in a variety of ways. At a very general level it is often seen as equivalent to a recognised and named major argument (for example, the 'Marxist paradigm'). Within the philosophy of science it has a more specific meaning, being equated with a way of thinking that sets out the dominant problems and solutions within a field.

Paradox A seemingly contradictory yet valid statement.

Plagiarism Most students understand that copying the words or the data of others without referencing their source is unacceptable. But what about the arguments of others? After all, most dictionaries include passing off the *thoughts* of others as one's own within their definition of plagiarism. If taken literally, this would both imply a required level of originality that is unobtainable and implicate most published work as plagiarised. The following three ground rules will help students clear their way through this potential minefield: a) As long as you are using your own words to convey an argument, placing all quoted material in quotation marks and referencing all secondary data, then you should not be accused of plagiarism. b) It is good practice to reference all arguments that are not your own. The more specific the argument and the less widely known, the more important this is. Conversely the more general and the more famous, the less vital it becomes. c) When in doubt err on the side of caution and reference your material.

Polemic A provocation; a one-sided and bullish argument. In academic life polemics are supposedly frowned upon yet remain quite common. They can sometimes be useful in starting a debate.

Populism Today usually a term of criticism, applied to views or practices deemed to be appealing not to reason or truth but to the sentiments of a mass audience.

Premise A starting point. To detail one's premises is to state what one is accepting, what one takes as given. Where the premise of a piece of work is introduced in this way we find phrases such as 'If we accept that ...' or 'This work builds on Brown's theory of ...'. It is good practice to make one's premises clear and open to inspection. Of course, since any piece of work relies on numerous premises, this is always a limited exercise. The uncovering of undeclared premises that undermine or otherwise compromise a piece of work can provide a useful form of criticism (see also **presupposition**).

Presupposition What has been assumed beforehand in order to arrive at a particular conclusion. Thus, identifying a presupposition involves 'working back' from a statement in order to find its undeclared premises.

Problematic This term has three meanings: a) The most common refers to the existence of a problem. In this sense something is problematic because it is questionable. Relatedly, to *problematise* something is to assert and/or show that it is questionable. b) The second meaning derives from philosophy but is now employed in many other disciplines. In philosophical terms a problematic refers to propositions that contain a claim that something is possible. c) The third meaning of problematic is often encountered in the social sciences. Although occasionally ambiguous in intent, this usage equates the term with a set of interconnected difficulties or questions (for example, 'the environmental problematic' or 'the racial problematic in British society').

Proof Generally speaking, a proof is a piece of evidence. However, the claim that one has proved something demands not merely evidence but *conclusive* evidence. In nearly all fields of inquiry, evidence that leaves no room for error and no possibility of doubt is usually difficult to obtain. Hence, claims to have proved something are often avoided or heavily qualified.

Proposition This term has two meanings: a) an assertion; b) a proposed scheme. The former meaning can provide a useful synonym for argument.

QED (Abbreviation of *quod erat demonstrandum*; Latin: that which was to be demonstrated). To write QED means one is claiming to have proved what one set out to prove. The term serves a function when appended to mathematical solutions but is rarely appropriate elsewhere.

Red herring Something (be it a fact, theory or methodology) that is irrelevant but distracting.

reductio ad absurdum (Latin: reduction to absurdity) A form of criticism in which one refutes a position by showing that to follow its logical consequences would lead to some form of absurdity (for example, illogicality).

Reductionism A term of criticism used to describe the act of explaining a complex process or event by reference to a misleadingly narrow range of causal factors (often the term's target is seen to have just one, crudely understood, explanatory principle).

Relativism The belief that truths are contingent and relational (cf. **universalism**). The relativist emphasises that this diversity should be acknowledged and respected but does not necessarily accept that all outcomes are of equal worth or value.

Research question Academic argument is about asking questions. Within most fields of inquiry it is useful to frame one's basic and, if appropriate, supplementary research questions at the beginning of a written or an oral presentation. Research questions encapsulate an inquiry in terms that enable and suggest evidence-based study. It is good practice to keep the number of research questions one poses to a minimum. This helps ensure one provides adequate responses to the questions one has asked.

Rhetoric This term was first used to refer to the art of effective argument. Ancient Greek and Roman teachers of rhetoric (*rhetor* is Greek for 'speaker in the assembly') divided the subject into five parts: invention, arrangement, style, memory and delivery. Although the original sense of the term was not confined to oral argument, much of the ancient meaning of the word is retained in the still common notion that 'good speakers' possess 'rhetorical skills'. However, aside from increasingly residual exceptions, the meaning of rhetoric has shifted from a positive to a negative evaluation. To the modern ear, to say something is rhetoric or rhetorical implies that, although it may be verbally and logically sophisticated, it is insincere and exaggerated.

Sexism Bias in favour of, or against, one sex.

Simile A figure of speech in which something is likened to something else. Similes use 'like' or 'as'. For example, 'Her argument was like a badly constructed building'.

Socratic method A form of dialogue employed (according to Plato) by Socrates. The dialogue is between teacher and pupil and involves the former patiently questioning the latter in such a way as to enable the pupil to recognise a true conclusion. Thus, rather than the pupil simply being told what the truth is, the Socratic method presumes that they already know the truth but require wise and enabling counsel in order to recognise it.

Solipsism The practice of construing one's own experience as the only reality. Solipsism is intellectually rooted in extreme relativism, i.e. a position that leads to a denial of any shared values or meanings between people. However, it is also commonly used as a term of criticism for any self-centred, self-absorbed argument.

Sophistry The art of deceptive and erroneous argument.

Straw man The practice of fabricating an artificial and easily assailed target. To accuse someone of constructing a straw man is a common criticism. It should not be used against arguments that are merely simplifying or addressing the essence of their target but, rather, at those that are presenting a misleading, ignorant and distorting caricature of it.

Structure The structure of an argument is its logical, theoretical and empirical framework. All arguments have some kind of structure. However, those that have clearly demarcated sections and a logical (for example, cumulative) construction tend to be more coherent and convincing. See Chapter 2 for discussion.

Subjective This word is usually equated with personal, individual reactions and perceptions (cf. **objective**). Social scientists wishing to account for the way meaning is often neither objective nor merely individual, but social and held in common, have also made use of terms such as 'inter-subjective' and 'social meaning'.

Syllogism A formal philosophical exercise in logic. A basic syllogism consists of two propositions, three terms and a conclusion. A classic example is 'All men are mortal; Greeks are men, therefore all Greeks are mortal'.

Synonym A word that has the same meaning as another.

Tautology A statement that repeats itself. The phrases 'They arrived one after the other in succession' and 'in two equal halves' are tautological. Although usually used in everyday speech to refer to clauses or short sentences, tautology can be identified within any type or length of communication. As a term of criticism it is particularly useful when addressing arguments that claim to be based on logical progression but are, in fact, products of the ability to say the same thing more than once using different words.

Teleology Sometimes called 'the design argument', teleology describes those explanations based on some ultimate overarching plan or structure. See Chapter 4 for discussion.

Theory A set of explanatory principles (cf. **methodology**). Theories are generic rather than particular (cf. **hypothesis**) and represent an attempt to discern or construct explanations at a relatively high level of abstraction. Thus, we talk of 'the theory of evolution' or 'the theory of structuration'. When the term theory is applied to specific, non-generalisable events (for example, 'The theory is that I wrote this book to help students') it is either being misused ('thesis' or 'proposition' would be better choices) or invoking the popular definition of theory as any speculative notion. See Chapters 1 and 2 for discussion.

Thesis A statement of fact (cf. **hypothesis**). A thesis is a truth claim. It is often used as a synonym for argument (i.e. 'The argument/thesis that I will be advancing in this paper …'). However, the term thesis carries the specific claim that its truthfulness will be evidenced (and, perhaps, proven) in what follows. Thus, if one starts a piece of work claiming one has a thesis it is important to make good that claim by showing it to be useful and accurate.

Universalism The belief that truths are true for everyone and are not context dependent (cf. **relativism**). The universalist emphasises the importance of uncovering these truths (often understood as laws) and arriving at generalisable conclusions.